Measuring and Maximizing Training Impact

Measuring and Maximizing Training Impact

Bridging the Gap between Training and Business Results

Paul Leone

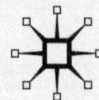

MEASURING AND MAXIMIZING TRAINING IMPACT
Copyright © Paul Leone, 2014.

All rights reserved.

First published in 2014 by
PALGRAVE MACMILLAN®
in the United States—a division of St. Martin's Press LLC,
175 Fifth Avenue, New York, NY 10010.

Where this book is distributed in the UK, Europe and the rest of the world, this is by Palgrave Macmillan, a division of Macmillan Publishers Limited, registered in England, company number 785998, of Houndmills, Basingstoke, Hampshire RG21 6XS.

Palgrave Macmillan is the global academic imprint of the above companies and has companies and representatives throughout the world.

Palgrave® and Macmillan® are registered trademarks in the United States, the United Kingdom, Europe and other countries.

ISBN: 978–1–137–41479–3

Library of Congress Cataloging-in-Publication Data

Leone, Paul.
  Measuring and maximizing training impact : bridging the gap between training and business results / Paul Leone.
    pages cm
  ISBN 978–1–137–41479–3 (alk. paper)
  1. Employees—Training of. 2. Organizational effectiveness. I. Title.

HF5549.5.T7L466 2014
658.3'124—dc23   2014006310

A catalogue record of the book is available from the British Library.

Design by Newgen Knowledge Works (P) Ltd., Chennai, India.

First edition: September 2014

10 9 8 7 6 5 4 3 2 1

Printed in the United States of America.

Contents

List of Illustrations   vii
Preface   xi

Introduction   Bridging the Gap between Training and Business Results   1
Chapter 1   Did They Like It?   17
Chapter 2   Did They Learn Anything?   27
Chapter 3   Are They Doing Anything Different?   37
Chapter 4   Did It Impact the Business?   73
Chapter 5   Was It Worth It?   103
Chapter 6   How Do We Maximize Impact?   117
Summary   151
Conclusion   161
Case Study 1   Measuring the Impact of Leadership Training   165
Case Study 2   Maximizing the Impact of Leadership Training through Different Delivery Modes   185

Index   199

Illustrations

Figures

0.1	"The Bridge"	4
1.1	Quantitative results for Level 1	24
1.2	How to show qualitative results for Level 1	24
1.3	Sample of Level 1 qualitative report	25
2.1	Quantitative results for Level 2	33
2.2	Qualitative results for Level 2	33
2.3	Overall snapshot report for Levels 1 and 2	35
3.1	The ROI of building your bridge (the business case)	49
3.2	Domain of Level 3 behaviors	53
3.3	Picking the right leadership behaviors for a Level 3	54
3.4	Cutting the crap	56
3.5	Response distribution for a Level 3 question	65
3.6	Aggregate slide for all Level 3 behaviors	68
3.7	Level 3 qualitative results from direct reports after a leadership training program	71
4.1	Level 4 analysis showing productivity differences between those who improved their behaviors (High Improvement) and those who did not (No Improvement)	87
4.2	Calculating the *effect*	89

4.3	Defining the "effected" population	92
4.4	Calculating your effect size	92
4.5	Level 4 showing differences in direct report productivity caused by improving leadership	98
4.6	Level 4 analysis for a leadership program	99
4.7	Example of Level 4 qualitative analysis	100
5.1	The ROI formula	104
5.2	Calculating your "benefit"	108
5.3	Calculating your "cost"	109
5.4	Calculating your cost	110
5.5	Return on investment	112
6.1	Three "make or break" climate factors	139
6.2	How do your top three factors discriminate between levels of impact?	141
6.3	Better climate = greater ROI	142
6.4	Target Impact Plan	147
6.5	Impact of TIP	148
S.1	The bridge	152
S.2	The measurement process	158
S.3	Final takeaways	159
CS1.1	The good leader profit chain	167
CS1.2	Level 1 results	172
CS1.3	Level 2 results	172
CS1.4	Level 3 results	174
CS1.5	Qualitative results for Level 3	175
CS1.6	Level 4 productivity differences	176
CS1.7	Calculating an overall effect size	179
CS1.8	Calculating the ROI for leadership training	180
CS1.9	Level 6—critical climate factors	182
CS2.1	Comparison of Level 1 and 2 scores	189

CS2.2	Comparison of Level 3 improvement	190
CS2.3	Calculating a Level 4 "effect size" for online training	191
CS2.4	Overall effect sizes compared across delivery modes	192

Tables

0.1	The traditional five levels of evaluation	14
0.2	Six levels of evaluation	15
1.1	Example of a Level 1 survey	23
2.1	Sample Level 2 survey	32
2.2	Levels 1 and 2 measuring levels of satisfaction and learning from training	34
3.1	Level 3 questions with improvement scale	64
6.1	Twelve factors for your climate assessment	124
6.2	The Transfer Climate Assessment	135
S.1	Measurement process, Levels 1 and 2	153
S.2	Measurement process, Levels 3–6	154
CS1.1	Six Levels of evaluation	168
CS2.1	Level 1–6 evaluation approach	187
CS2.2	Training benefits across delivery modes	193
CS2.3	Benefits, costs, and final ROI results for each delivery mode	195

Preface

Why Measure?

Organizations in the United States alone spend over $150 billion on training and employee development every year. With that type of investment, coupled with the intense focus and unflinching scrutiny most businesses place on the bottom line, one would naturally assume that the "payoff" or ultimate benefits (e.g., increased productivity and revenue) of all these training programs are being rigorously measured and monetized down to the last penny. Surprisingly, this assumption could not be further from the truth. One of the biggest conundrums in the corporate world today is why organizations are not measuring the business returns on these colossal training expenditures. Even the most bottom-line–minded businesses, the ones that pinch and squeeze every penny to show profitable growth year over year, seem to be oddly accepting and complacent with their inability to demonstrate an aggressive return on their training investments. In fact, the vast majority of organizations don't even take the most fundamental steps to determine if the training is even "working." That is, does it actually improve the knowledge, skills, and performance it was designed to improve? Are employees more productive than they were before the training? Are they doing *anything* different back on the job?

Granted, turning all the benefits of training into solid, top-line dollar values is no easy task, but most organizations don't even try. They collect little or no data to connect training events to employee behavior, they collect no data connecting employee behavior to business results, and they certainly never come close to building a sound ROI case for their training investments. When we look at the magnitude of these training budgets compared to the amount of comprehensive impact studies that are being done, we are instantly faced with the irrefutable fact that otherwise smart, savvy, profit-focused organizations are sending millions of employees through training experiences, spending billions of dollars on training every year, and quite literally have nothing to show for it.

You don't need to be a finance guru to know that without some visible and tangible benefits on the top line you're always going to have a disappointing and dismal bottom line. Instead of focusing on the value added by the training, business leaders and stakeholders will always be forced to focus on what they can see and touch—the expense of training. After all, the only thing they have in front of their faces are the costs. And to make matters even more challenging, companies have always gone to, and will continue to go to, great lengths to define all their costs in exhaustive and excruciating detail. So, using the simplest benefits to costs ratio analysis (BCR), what almost all organizations end up with are some very vague or absent numbers above the line and some very real and punishing numbers below the line. What kind of ROI case can you make with this data? If we ever want senior executives to think of training as a profitable business imperative, instead of a distractive and costly diversion, we need to define these benefits in detail, monetize them, and create powerful stories of impact and ROI. Put simply, we need to give them "something to show for it."

The conspicuous absence of these tangible returns and the credible data supporting them is the fundamental reason why training gets a bad rap. Employees and their sponsors are literally dropping thousands of precious dollars (money that can certainly be spent on far more tangible and attractive goods or services) on a training experience that seemingly offers no predictable and quantifiable payoffs. When everything is said and done, the vendors or trainers go home with all the money, and the trainees go home with empty pockets and empty hands (except perhaps for a wonderful, giant, loose-leaf binder that won't see daylight again until ten years later when they're cleaning out their desks). Not only that, but these employees just spent all day away from their real jobs, where they would have been making real and expected contributions to the bottom line. This leads to an adversarial relationship between the training groups (including HR) who develop and put out the training program and the business functions who most often foot the bill for all of their employees. In fact, in this scenario, any type of employee development initiative can quickly be lumped in and viewed as yet another wasteful endeavor that yanks employees away from their everyday roles driving business results.

Imagine walking into a retail store, a shop, a restaurant, or a showroom, spending thousands of dollars, and then walking away empty-handed. Very few of us would be comfortable with that. As part of our evolution as a collective civilization, we have grown to depend on an age-old, tried and true system of bartering and reciprocity for our survival and security. In other words, when we spend money or resources on anything, we are accustomed to and have absolutely come to expect something back in return. Obviously, we have evolved and learned to accept some level of delayed gratification (e.g., the return on a college degree), but nevertheless, we still do very much expect to be apprised of and to ultimately enjoy the more tangible benefits (e.g., a higher paying job) somewhere down the road. Further, when we give something as tangible and valuable as cold hard cash, we certainly expect to walk away from that transaction with something just as tangible, and quite often, even more valuable. It typically should be something we can hold in our hands, wear on our bodies, or park in our driveways.

Without tangible benefits handed out, or at least promised in the near future, there will always be a lingering question (or doubt) about what something is truly worth. Here's an example: Would you rather go offsite to a two-day leadership training program or purchase a vacation package to Venice? It sounds like a silly question, right? We'd all choose the vacation. But why do we smirk and really think it's such a silly question? If we truly believed that the training "worked" and would make us better, more productive leaders, wouldn't it be the right investment? After all, being a better leader could surely lead to a promotion in the near future, and that could mean an increase of $20,000 in annual salary. This could mean ten trips to Europe! The real problem is that deep down, we may all harbor a little skepticism over the ultimate payoff of training and that's because we've never been bombarded (or even slightly peppered) with the evidence of impact and ROI.

So what's the problem? Why do employees and their businesses end up with nothing to show for this multibillion dollar investment? Why aren't organizations making an aggressive and determined attempt to measure and report the true benefits of their training programs? The short answer is simple—they lack the expertise and confidence to present their results to senior business leaders. In a recent study, it was estimated that over 95 percent of organizations feel the real need and urgency to demonstrate the impact and bottom-line value of training, but less than 5 percent feel confident in their ability to measure and report that very same business impact. The paradox here is that ROI numbers are so important to the business that most training organizations are too afraid to present them. They want to get it right so bad, and they are so deathly afraid of getting it wrong, that they end up presenting nothing! This paralysis and lack of data is quickly interpreted as ineffectiveness and only fuels the already prevalent notion, especially amidst the more skeptical business leaders, that most employees' training doesn't "work" and is simply a frivolous waste of time and money.

Ironically, another reason why HR and training groups are not doling out the impact studies is that they have historically been given somewhat of a "free pass" when it comes to proving their worth and justifying their expenses. Because they represent, advocate, and spend much of their resources on developing the human side of the business, organizational leaders tend to be cautious about taking them to task and demanding irrefutable evidence that every single one of their initiatives are turning a profit. No leader wants to advance the notion that investing in people is a "bad" idea. Giving even the slightest hint or inkling that you don't want to develop and enrich your employees can surely put you on the fast track to early *unpaid* retirement. As most leaders realize, *human capital* and *capital gains* are better kept in separate conference rooms. While this historical treatment has been a blessing on the one hand, it may also have, over the years, rendered us just a little bit more relaxed when it comes to proving our value to the business. And although the burning platform has surely been ignited by the incredible and groundbreaking work of the Phillips and the Kirkpatricks, the sheer lack of fire for so many years has simply left most training organizations inexperienced at the art and science of defining their worth.

When you put these two factors together (lack of confidence and no experience), you end up with an inevitable scenario where

HR and its internal training groups are just not able to compete for resources as well as most of the other functions throughout the organization. Organizational leaders and stakeholders must allocate their limited capital and make hard decisions about where they want to invest their money. It should come as no surprise that they will be focused on what will provide the largest and surest return on their investments. Obviously, the business groups and functions that can show a great ROI track record and present their budgetary needs with the promise of demonstrable returns will be the ones getting the lion's share of resources.

The funny thing is most of the other parts of the organization don't have their ROI calculations down to a perfect science either. In fact, they use many of the same types of methods to identify their impact (i.e., baseline vs. postlaunch comparisons, feedback, estimations, trend analyses, and projections, etc.) as we do. The only big difference is they have become relatively confident and versed in presenting their ROI cases. For their own survival, they are quick and adept at summing up their contributions, defining their worth and aggressively taking their share of the credit when the company sees any improvements in business performance. For example, if a marketing group puts out a new ad campaign or a nationally broadcasted commercial and then for two months postlaunch there is a significant spike in sales revenue, they are very quick to attribute this growth to the genius of the ad. Similarly, if technology puts out a new portal for employees to access customer information faster and more securely, and then for three months after that customer satisfaction metrics soar, the tech group is quick to take all the credit.

If you notice, in both of these scenarios, the rigor of the research did not go much beyond looking at the trending of the metrics (baseline) and the timing of the initiative (launch). From these methods they calculate the aggregate monetary benefits of their productivity jumps and then an ROI case is presented. Does that sound like a perfectly objective science? Have they really controlled for all the factors that could have caused an increase in business performance? Have they truly isolated the influence of their initiative and parsed out the effect size to a statistical certainty? Of course not! But what they have done is *some* research and they *did* bother to put together a business case. And that gets heads nodding in their direction when it's time for top executives to allocate budgets. And even though it's far from perfect, do you think there would be much debate or question about the data and the ultimate estimate of ROI?

The point is this, we can never effectively compete for resources, or the respect we deserve at the C-table, if we bring no proof of our contributions. Imagine going for a job and submitting a resume with no previous accomplishment, no clear description of the value you will add, and then in large, bold print—your salary requirements? Can you imagine going to a bank and asking a loan officer for money to open a new business and promising nothing in return? Can you imagine going in front of a judge to plead your case and presenting no hard evidence? In all these cases, you'd either be laughed at, asked to leave, or escorted to the door. While I exaggerate a bit, the reality is when we don't present any benefits of training and employee development, we leave top executives and decision-makers little choice but to dismiss our requests for higher spending and drop us to the bottom of their priority list.

If you're not too disturbed about relinquishing your fair share of corporate spending, think about what happens to these low priority groups when organizations have to really tighten their belts. In a bleak economy, those groups who can't show (with real numbers) that they are absolutely critical to business success put themselves in a very dangerous place. Consider this scenario: You're a CEO making decisions on which groups to target for cutbacks and layoffs. You have four portfolios of year-end accomplishments in front of you. You open the first from Marketing and you see "Estimated revenue generated from new TV commercial—$18 million." You open the second from Technology and see "Expected cost savings over the next 3 years from integrating new internet platform—$11 million." You open the next from Sales and read "Additional revenue from new accounts—38.4 million." Then you get to HR Training and you open it up and there before you it says, "We helped." What would you do if you had to reduce headcount for one of these groups?

The ultimate message here is—you must do your business impact and ROI studies. Do you need to have a credible research methodology yielding valid and reliable results? Of course. Do you need a dissertation that proves a statistical effect size down to the final decimal? No. While you're taking years to design the perfect and unchallengeable study, the rest of your organization is presenting their less-rigorous ROI cases, getting every bit of the budget they need, and establishing their reputation as a critical contributor to business survival. If you want a seat at the table, you can't be afraid to present your results. Even if your ROI is estimated as a range (150—200 percent) because you haven't worked out all the kinks, putting something out there is better than putting out nothing at all. You'll be surprised how appreciative business leaders are to see that you're linking your initiatives to the metrics they really care about. They're not looking for perfection—they just want to hear from us. I remember when I first started conducting and presenting these impact studies over 12 years ago. I was far less confident and the reports were far less polished. But even then I remember how excited and receptive top executives were to see any type of ROI estimates coming from the training groups that were historically dead silent. Take my word for it—invest some resources into measuring your results and presenting your findings—it will be the best investment you ever make.

I hope I've made my case for measuring the impact of training. My purpose for writing this book is to encourage you to measure your impact and present your results. Once you have a measurement strategy in place, you'll not only be able to report how your training worked in the past tense, but you'll be able to describe how to make your training more effective in the future. That is, when you understand all the cause and effect linkages between the original training event and the final business results, you can then uncover all the factors that most profoundly influence its impact back on the job. Once you build this bridge between training and business performance, you'll be able to make any training program you measure more effective. Simply put, *measuring your training impact will maximize your training impact*.

INTRODUCTION

Bridging the Gap between Training and Business Results

The "Bridge"

Why is it that when we put two comparable individuals through the exact same training program, one might show an incredible return on investment while the other shows no change, no business impact, and ultimately yields a fantastic waste of time and money?

Both participants begin at the same starting point (e.g., investment, training content, mode of delivery, etc.) and both set their sights on the same destination (higher productivity, greater revenue, etc.). So what goes wrong along the way? Why is one participant's journey from training to business results so smooth and spectacular, while the other falters and plummets to an early, dismal demise? The answer is simple—they crossed dramatically different "bridges."

Like any bridge, there are critical support factors that allow us to transfer and traverse safely across to our destination. If constructed carelessly, the bridge crumbles under us, causing us to plummet and flail in the treacherous waters below. As expert architects in any industry, it's up to us to find out what makes these bridges strong and design their structures accordingly. What are the building blocks and linkages that connect our bridge? What are the environmental or "climate" factors that strengthen or, in many cases, threaten their integrity? And what type of support structures are going to hold up our bridge through the harshest of climates?

For training and performance architects, the question is: How do employees cross this bridge and what are the critical climate factors that most affect their journey? What's in their immediate work environment (when they return to their desks, workspaces, etc.) that either helps or hinders their "transfer" of learning from the training event (their point of origin) to on-the-job business results (their destination)? Once identified, these climate factors become the dramatic support beams that drive deep into the ground, hold up our bridge, and, quite literally, make or break all our training programs.

What Does This Bridge Look Like?

So what does this whole bridge actually look like? Well, like any bridge, there are two fundamental parts: the horizontal path that stretches across from one side to the other, and the vertical support pillars that actually hold up this path.

The Path

The path begins where the participant's journey begins—with the training event. If the training engages the employee, he can take the first step. If the employee learns something new, he can take another step. If the footing is sure enough, and he ends up doing something different or better on the job, he can take one more step and continue on his journey. If this behavior change leads to improved productivity, yet another step can be taken. And finally, if this improved productivity impacts the bottom line and outweighs the cost of the training, the participant has stayed the course, reached his destination, and finished his dangerous journey.

When it comes to building this clear and unobstructed path, it is our responsibility as architects to make sure it's pointed in the right direction, the employee has a clear line of sight to the destination, and the stepping stones are tightly linked together. For instance, we need to define how new learning will affect behavior, which behaviors will change after training, how those behaviors will lead to productivity improvements, and so on. And most of all, we need to measure the strength of all these steps and linkages along the way. If something veers employees off their path and they never arrive at their destination, we'll know where the journey faltered and failed.

The Pillars

The other part of the bridge, which I consider even more critical, are the huge support pillars that actually hold it up. While the path allows employees to put one foot in front of the other and move in the right direction, the support structures underlying that path are what keep them from plummeting into the empty, dark abyss below. These pillars ultimately allow an employee to take each and every crucial step of the journey. If these can't stand the test of time and endure all the "inclement" conditions that threaten them, the whole bridge crumbles and the employee's journey comes to an abrupt and wasteful end.

The bridge I've just described is actually designed, constructed, and traversed by measuring and defining the traditional five levels of impact (the path) and then adding a new, sixth level (the pillars) (see figure 0.1). What I'm going to do in this book is take you on a journey across this bridge. And by the end of this book, you will be able to build your own incredible, majestic bridge! I'm going to show you how to create and measure each step along the way. I'm going to tell you how to construct the right linkages and measure the impact of your training programs from the first step (Level 1—Participant

4 • Measuring and Maximizing Training Impact

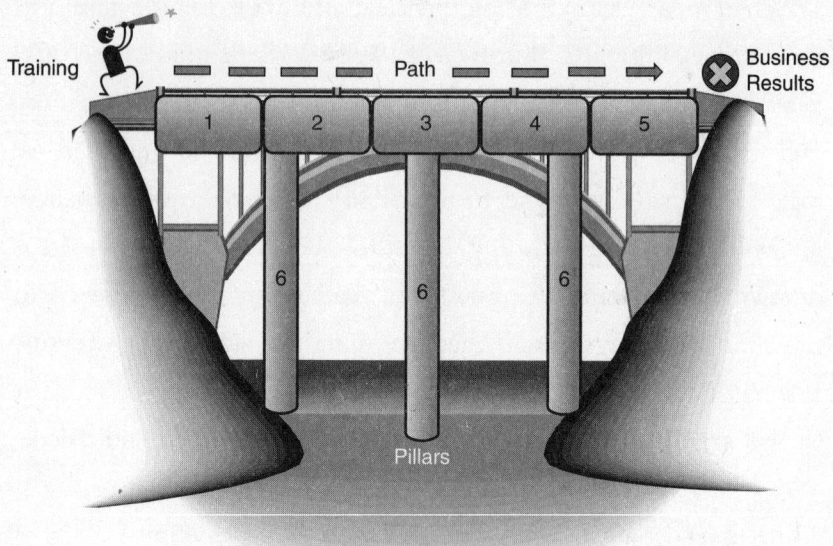

Figure 0.1 "The Bridge."

Satisfaction) to the final one (Level 5—Return on Investment). And most importantly, I'm going to help you create a new Level 6, which measures the critical factors that surround and support your bridge, and can truly make or break all your training initiatives. The best part about all this is I'm going to show you some new, simple, and practical ways to do all six levels. Get ready to make a huge impact to the bottom line because without a strong, sturdy bridge in place, your employees will never reach their destination and your training will never impact the business. So, don't waste another penny on training until you build your bridge.

Did Someone Say "Evaluation Level 6"?

After many years of conducting impact studies with tens of thousands of trainees, I came to one rather conspicuous conclusion: you can't measure the true effectiveness of training until you know what the climate is like. And you can't figure out what the right climate is like until you know how to measure training impact. Because the effectiveness of training cannot be measured in a vacuum, without also evaluating the climate that influences that effectiveness, I've added what I call a Level 6 "transfer climate" to the traditional five levels of evaluation.

While the traditional five levels are absolutely critical to any evaluation strategy, they don't give you the fullest picture of training success or failure and leave out what I believe to be the most dynamic part of the story. That is, they tell you whether training "worked" or didn't work in the past tense, but don't offer any quantitative findings describing how to maximize that impact and make the same training more successful in the future.

Additionally, a Level 6 can explain the variability of training effectiveness across the organization. It arms you as the training professional with a critical narrative for your business clients—why does training work for Mary and not for Joe? By uncovering and explaining this type of variability in training effectiveness, you are able to inform your business partners what *they* can do differently as business leaders to drive and maximize their own training dollars. They are the ones who can create and drive the right "transfer climates" for Mary and Joe back on the job. After all, leaders spend a lot of money putting their employees through training—isn't it only fair that they have some control over the outcome?

In all my years of presenting Level 1–6 evaluation results, I have yet to encounter a business group that does not find the results about their transfer climate the most interesting and informative piece of the presentation. When I tell my audience I'm giving them Level 1–5 results for their training, of course they're excited—less than 4 percent of all companies are doing it and even less do it right. But when I tell them I'm also giving them quantitative Level

6 results to explain why training succeeds or fails back on the job, that's what really gets them to the edge of their seats. Imagine being able to say to your business partners, "We understand this training was more effective for some employees than others, we know why it was more effective, and this is what you can do to make it more effective in the future." Now which business leader wouldn't be happy with that little tidbit? Welcome to Level 6. OK, enough with the introductions—we have a beautiful bridge to build, so let's get building, shall we?

Building Your Bridge

Training is where the journey begins, but it's crossing the bridge to the desired outcome that makes any initiative successful. Each employee must be able to make this treacherous journey on his own, but we as architects can do some things to help them along the way. We can create a clear and smooth path to their destination, identify the most influential climate factors, and build strong support pillars to endure that climate and ensure everything doesn't crumble under their feet.

This is how we build our bridge.

Create a Clear Path

Far too often, training groups will choose a solution, highlight the key learning objectives, and then "hope" that it will have an impact on the business "somewhere down the line." This stab-in-the-dark approach becomes glaringly obvious when those same training groups are asked to present their business case and evidence of impact after the training is launched. They all end up scrambling under the gun (or axe) to convince their business partners with a few smile sheets and anecdotal testimonials that the training "worked." This approach to training evaluation is so ill-conceived, so inadequate, and at the same time so prevalent that it completely undermines all the hard work we do as training professionals. It never allows us to demonstrate with powerful methods and robust data that training is in fact having an incredible impact on the health and profitability of the business. To leaders and bottom-line-minded professionals, this ill-fated approach only perpetuates the perception of training as more of a diversion, instead of a true business imperative.

This is where building a solid evaluation strategy comes in. With a rigorous, but practical measurement approach, you will be able to not only build your business case up front, but also assess that same business case after the training is over. A good evaluation strategy proposes clear cause and effect linkages (e.g., how will new behaviors affect an employee's business metrics, etc.) before the training is even launched. The only thing that should be done post-training is actually testing the strength of those linkages and calculating the amount of impact at each level.

When it comes to creating this evaluation strategy and building your business case, just keep it simple and intuitive. A good way to approach it is to start at your destination and work your way backward. That is, begin with the business results you need to change or improve and ask yourself what employee behaviors need to change in order for that business impact to happen. Then, what type of employee learning will create that behavior change? And finally, what kind of training will embed that specific chunk of learning in my employees? Believe me, outlining these linkages and relationships up front is a fairly simple step that will make all the difference later on.

For this reason, I'm going to spend chapters 1–5 of this book walking you through a simple, quick, and practical way to measure all five traditional levels of evaluation and show you how easy it can be to set up your own comprehensive measurement strategy. I'll show you a new way to identify your key behaviors (Level 3), and give you a new, powerful method to isolate and quantify your business impact (Level 4). And don't worry, I'll give you all the resources and examples you'll need to do it yourself.

This is how you create your path.

Build Your Support Pillars

Imagine going through years of training to learn how to ski and then on the day of your first downhill competition, it doesn't snow. Imagine going to batting practice day after day and then your coach sits you on the bench. And imagine training your heart out to be the best defensive tackle on your team and then they only pay the quarterback. How motivated would you be to apply your training and improve your performance? The fact is, to really demonstrate any new learning and/or skills you acquire in training, certain environmental conditions always need to be met.

Now imagine going through training at work and going back to an environment that doesn't support the application and demonstration of that training. What if your everyday job role doesn't afford you the opportunity to apply it? What if your leader doesn't care about the training or your development? What if there are no rewards (formal or informal) for changing and improving your behaviors? The fact is, there are many "climate" factors that can foster or frustrate the impact of your training, so it's up to us as architects to identify which have the biggest influence and improve them. What are the biggest supporters and most significant predictors of success?

Because work environments, business, groups, and success metrics can be incredibly diverse within and across organizations, these climate factors and support pillars are not universal and "set in stone." There are many possible factors that exist within your own unique organizations and uncovering them will take a bit of research and analysis. However, the good news is that I'm going to show you exactly how to identify your own unique climate factors. And the return on that fairly simple analysis will prove to be one of the best investments you'll ever make.

Once you've done your analysis and surfaced a set of critical factors, you're then ready to build a tool or process that addresses and precisely targets those very factors. You're ready to partner with your business leaders and develop a solution that brings the biggest predictors of success to life. These solutions or tools usually include highlighting what the climate factors are, what the role of participant and leader will be in improving these climate elements, and a "contract" on what "improvement" would look like three months down the road. While the entire process takes very little "extra" energy, follow-up results clearly show that a few of these deliberate and prescriptive actions along the way can significantly improve your climate.

So, in chapter 6, I will summarize and share the results of my own research in the past decade and show you exactly how to do your own Level 6 evaluation. I will provide you with a post-training assessment tool I call the Transfer Climate Assessment. This assessment includes all the "usual suspects" (strongest factors) I've identified over the years. From this assessment, through an iterative process, you'll be able to hone in on your three most powerful factors. Then, I'll show you how to create a simple and practical tool to target your three factors and foster successful behavior change and sustained impact. I'll also show you the powerful results of implementing this type of simple solution. Finally, at the end of this book I'll walk you through a two-part case study that brings all of these evaluation levels to life and show you just how much climate can influence your training outcomes. Through these impact studies, you'll see that building a solid support structure to address your top three factors and "warming" your climate just a little will surely produce bountiful returns on your training dollars.

This is how you build your pillars.

Evaluating Levels 1–6

To build our bridge, complete with path and pillars, we have to evaluate our training from Levels 1 to 6. After all, to accurately predict and distinguish the training "successes" from the training "failures," you first have to define training impact (Level 1–5), and then the training climate that influences that impact (Level 6). But don't panic! Creating your evaluation strategy and building your bridge is much easier than it sounds. And I'll be holding your hand the whole way across. Before we take our first steps, here's a quick review of the five levels we'll be covering in the following chapters, as well as a quick preview of Level 6.

The Traditional Five

Probably the most well-known and widest used measures of training impact are those set forth by Kirkpatrick and Phillips (Level 1–5). These levels define the effects of training from a participant's initial reaction to the course (typically measured immediately after the event) all the way through to its effect on the bottom line (measured months after completion to allow for a participant to apply his/her learning and experience on the job). The five levels and what they evaluate are summed up in the following sections.

Level 1: Reaction and Satisfaction
Did they like it? Level 1 measures the extent to which training participants react positively to the training. Were they engaged? Was it

worth their time? Were they satisfied with the design, the content, and the way it was delivered? Level 1 may also include questions about relevance to the job and a participant's intent to apply the training. The Level 1 surveys are typically administered immediately after the program to capture impressions while they are still fresh. They may also ask participants for open-ended or qualitative feedback (e.g., "What would you do to improve this training?" or "What was the best/worst part of this training experience?"). How these Level 1 results are used may vary widely across (or even within) organizations. Some give the data a cursory glance and off it goes to a desolate database, while others analyze and scrutinize the data, reading through each comment to find ways they can improve the delivery of their training in the future.

Level 2: Learning and Skill Acquisition
Did they learn anything? Level 2 measures the extent to which new knowledge and skills were acquired during the training. Are they leaving with critical knowledge and capabilities that will help them do their jobs better? This may also include an attitude change or a new way of looking at an issue or problem. The data here tell us whether they have acquired something valuable that gives them the "potential" to perform better, but it stops there. Although we hope that it predicts improved behaviors and performance on the job, there's no way of knowing how this new learning affects their performance until after the employees are back on the job and higher levels of data can be collected. Level 2 can take a few different forms. It may be a knowledge check at the end of the program, a difference score between a pre- and a post-test, or it can simply be a few questions asking participants to describe their acquired knowledge or skills in some quantitative (rating) or qualitative format ("What was your biggest piece of learning?") The Level 2 assessment is also

administered immediately after the program while the learning is still fresh. Again, how the results are used and reported can vary widely across organizations.

Level 3: Behavior Change and Application
Are they doing anything different? Level 3 measures the extent to which participants are returning to their everyday jobs and actually applying what they learned in training. Do they do something better? Do they do something more effectively or more efficiently? Level 3 is probably the most critical measure because if behavior change doesn't happen and nothing gets applied, then all the training impact stops there. No business metric improvement could ever be attributed to the training and certainly no ROI could ever be calculated. Conversely, if you can demonstrate that your training improved the way employees do something, you're literally "half way there." The behavioral or performance improvements can then be quantified and analyzed to see if they predict increases in the critical metrics that matter most to the business. Level 3 typically comes in the form of a survey administered 2 to 4 months after the training concludes. Quantitative rating scales and qualitative open-ended questions are used to collect the necessary data. Organizations that do Level 3 may vary somewhat in their methods and designs, but ultimately collect and report on levels of improvement in key competencies and on-the-job capabilities.

Level 4: Business Impact
Did it impact the business? Level 4 measures the extent to which training is improving critical business metrics. That is, did the behavioral improvements and applying the new knowledge and skills actually lead to better business metrics and higher performance? What was the increase in productivity? What was the increase in sales revenue,

customer satisfaction, or amount of widgets produced? What were the real benefits to the business? Level 4 is where data collection becomes more challenging—or should I say, collecting the "right" data becomes more challenging. Here is where you want to say with both correlation and a certain degree of causation that your Level 3 behavior changes actually predict your Level 4 business results. Here is where you need to identify the most important metrics to the business, define how much they improved, and then isolate how much of that improvement was directly attributable to your specific training program. Level 4 data are typically collected by partnering closely with the business and honing in on only those metrics that truly drive the success of the company. These data, like in Level 3, must be collected several months after the program to allow time for transfer and effect. Historically, some of the biggest challenges have been collecting the metrics and applying the right methods and research designs to isolate the impact of the training program. While great strides have been made, convincing senior business leaders and executives of these isolated "benefits" has been a tough sell. Hopefully, the new Level 4 design and analysis I introduce in this book will change that.

Level 5: ROI

Was it worth the investment? Level 5 measures the extent to which the "benefits" of a particular training experience outweigh the "costs" of that training experience. The final ROI is expressed as a percentage of the original investment. The ROI calculation can only be done when the benefits identified in Level 4 have been turned into dollar values for the business or monetized. Once monetized, they can then be compared to the total costs that have also all been monetized. The challenge here is that costs of training are so much more accessible and far more easily monetized than the benefits. The costs of training are either right there in front of you (via vendor invoices, registration fees, and airline reservations) or you may have to do a few small calculations (time away from job, etc.). On the other hand, the benefits are derived from the translation of productivity and performance metrics into dollar values. Not only that, but remember the research design needs to tease out just how much of that dollar value was due to the training. This creates a glaring disparity between the acceptance and credibility of the objective numbers (costs) compared to the acceptance and credibility of the more subjective ones (benefits). This imbalance is why the vast (and I do mean vast) majority of organizations never even come close to reporting at this level.

A snapshot of these five levels is presented in Table 0.1.

As you can see, measuring impact at each of these levels gets progressively more sophisticated as you move from Level 1 to 5. Level 1 is the easiest to quantify while Level 5 needs far more analysis and interpretation. An even more important distinction as you move from one level to the next is that the information in your report becomes exponentially more interesting, valuable, and critical to your business clients. For instance, think of the last training you received and just ask yourself these simple questions:

1. "Did I like the training?" Level 1
2. "Did I learn anything?" Level 2
3. "Did I change my behavior when I returned to my job?" Level 3
4. "Did changing my behavior make me more productive?" Level 4
5. "Was it worth the investment?" Level 5

Table 0.1 The traditional five levels of evaluation

Measurement	Evaluates...
Level 1	Reaction and satisfaction
Level 2	New knowledge acquired
Level 3	Behavior change/application
Level 4	Business impact/productivity increase
Level 5	Return on investment

Now imagine you were a business leader paying for five thousand employees to attend this training. Can you see how you might become increasingly more interested in the answers to these questions as you progress from Level 1 to 5?

New Level 6

So what would be the next question? What could be even more interesting and valuable than ROI? Well, what if your business leaders are planning on sending more employees through the same type of training in the future? Should we just tell them, "These are the results you can expect from training—have a nice day"? Or, could we take this opportunity to really WOW them and tell them HOW to improve their results and maximize their training dollars next week, next month, and next year?

A "Level 6" climate evaluation allows you to do just that. It builds on the traditional five levels of training evaluation and adds what I consider the most critical part of the story—what factors in the trainees' work environment will help or hinder training impact? I see it as the most critical because results of this additional level of analysis can ultimately tell you how to improve the impact and ROI of "any" training program within your organization. See table 0.2 with the new level added.

Okay, all refreshed and up to speed on the six levels we'll be covering? Just remember, by the end of this book, you'll be able to

Table 0.2 Six levels of evaluation

Measurement	Evaluates
Level 1	Reaction and satisfaction
Level 2	New knowledge acquired
Level 3	Behavior change/improvement
Level 4	Business impact/productivity increase
Level 5	Return on investment
Level 6	Climate factors maximizing impact

clearly, concisely, and confidently report each one. You'll get all the examples, templates, and sample reports you'll need. And of course I'll share some of the major DOs and DON'Ts I've learned over the years. You WILL build your own bridge. And I'll make it so simple it won't hurt a bit—I promise.

CHAPTER 1

Did They Like It?

How to Collect, Analyze, and Report Level 1 Data

Level 1 data, which captures employees' reaction and satisfaction with a training experience, is collected by at least 70 percent of all organizations that offer employee training programs and curricula. It provides a way to measure engagement and get an overall impression of the employee experience. While fairly simple and unscientific, it is a great way to get an initial read on the face validity and relevance of the training content. It also serves as an opportunity to gather initial feedback on what's working or not working in terms of design, duration, and facilitator effectiveness. These initial results will allow you to tweak your training design, approach, and/or content, and perhaps inform your trainers how to keep their audiences more engaged.

While there are endless possible questions you can include depending on what your initial goals are, there are only five core questions that you really need to ask:

1. Are you satisfied with the content (engaging materials, exercises, discussions, etc.)?
2. Are you satisfied with the delivery (facilitator or other delivery mode)?

3. What are the best and worst parts? (open-ended)
4. Overall, are you satisfied with the experience?
5. Would you recommend it to others?

With some version of these short and sweet questions you will be able to gather what you need to develop your full Level 1 report. Remember, a lot of Level 1 is good information to have, but why waste your time, and more importantly your survey-taker's time, when the results are not necessarily predictive of higher levels of impact. If you are indeed reporting up to Levels 3, 4, 5, and especially 6, these early levels become far less important and will fast be forgotten as you present your more comprehensive analyses. So keep it short. Here's a quick summary of why I included these five items:

1. Are you satisfied with the content (engaging materials, exercises, discussions, etc.)?
   If the materials are dull, outdated, or incomplete, the best magician or wittiest comedian couldn't keep the audience engaged and awake for more than an hour no less a whole day. That's why it's important to ask this question, but the big mistake many organizations make here is trying to hit on every possible thing that could be right or wrong with the training. If you try to cover every nuance of the training, you'll end up with a list of about 25 questions ranging from "Did you get all the materials?" to "How did you like Module 5 Section 8?" This is not going to endear you to your survey-takers and you're certainly not going to create a spirit of cooperation. Just keep it simple. Ask them if they're satisfied with the training content and give them the option of "Yes" or "No." If it's a "No," give them an opportunity to vent about the one big

problem they had with it. If you ask it 25 different ways and want 25 different ratings, they'll be checking off boxes just to get the heck out of there. Then you'll get no valuable data back. There's no use wasting their time and yours (remember you have to analyze all this stuff) if you could nail it all down with one question.

2. Are you satisfied with the way the training was delivered (facilitator, online experience, etc.)?

Here's your opportunity to fire that obnoxious orator who shows up late, falls asleep during breakout discussions, and clearly has no idea what he or she is talking about. Granted, these cases are extremely rare and facilitator ratings almost never veer away from their overwhelmingly positively skew, but we really still need to ask the question. While the question will never add up to any informative robust data, it's still important to detect that 1 in 50 cases where the instructor is truly murdering the chances of participants gaining anything valuable from the experience. This is why most vendors and training organizations insist on keeping it in their Level 1. If you are delivering the training online or using other media, the aggregate results become a little more actionable. Here, you can uncover things like technology issues and challenges that can have a widespread effect on your learners. Even if you're using multiple modes of delivery within one training program, you can still cover it all with one question. Whatever delivery modes you are using, get the "Yes" or "No" and let them add their specific color commentary if they feel the need to do so. If they have the facilitator from hell, you'll hear about it. If they couldn't log on to your system, you'll hear about it. If they don't call it out here, it probably wasn't that important in the first place.

3. **What are the best and worst parts?** (open-ended)

   If ever they had an opportunity to highlight something important, this is it. This is where you'll get some good feedback on the drivers and detractors of participant engagement. I've seen many programs evolve and improve based on these responses. For instance, in one training program a vast majority of participants said they loved the table discussions with their peers and benefited from the networking. Analyzing and really hearing that feedback, the vendor went off and worked several more table discussions into the training design for the following year. Similarly, one web-based training program received a huge number of negative responses pointing to the scenarios included in simulation training. The vendor made sure to rewrite the scripts and enhance all the scenarios for the next rollout. If you're open to and looking for opportunities to upgrade your training, pay close attention to these comments.

4. **Overall, are you satisfied with the experience?**

   This is purely "Yes" or "No" without any additional comments. I keep this question for one reason and one reason only—to summarize my Level 1 quantitative data. That is, if someone wants a quick snapshot of how all participants reacted to the training, this data point is what I use. As you'll see (hopefully) when you're reporting later on, your stakeholders are going to want a quick slide or a few brief bullets on Level 1 and then it's onto the more comprehensive and informative parts of your impact story. This is why you want a broad enough question to cover all levels of satisfaction. You don't want to be forced to look across all questions and comments and pull together some quantitative average. The response distribution to this question will give you that one headline you need for future reporting (e.g., "Overall, 92 percent of participants were satisfied with the training experience").

5. <u>Would you recommend it to others?</u>

This one I like because it provides some variability. In my experience, participants tend to be a little less generous with this question than with many others I've seen on Level 1. For instance, participants might give rave reviews to facilitators and sing praises of how great the content was, but when it comes to recommending the training to a coworker, they suddenly become a little more critical. Saying you'd recommend a training program to your peers says a lot more about the power of that experience than simply saying you are satisfied. Because of this greater variability, it's a good measure to track if you are continuously making changes and upgrades to your training program.

Scaling All Your Survey Questions

When it comes to developing a great, concise evaluation story, something that is almost as critical as the questions themselves is the scale or response options you provide your survey-takers. I will return to this important topic throughout the book because a little strategy and forethought about scaling will really change the power and impact of your reporting. What seems like small-scale nuances and petty "word-smithing" now can vastly improve the flow and impact of your results presentation later on.

For now, here are my three rules of thumb on building your actual scales:

1. <u>Don't use a neutral option in your sca</u>le. One of the most mystifying things to me is the amount of scales found across surveys, organizations, and even disciplines that include the

infamous "no opinion" or "neither agree nor disagree" right smack in the middle of the scale. For the sake of your data analysis, make your raters commit one way or another. How can you go through hours or days of a training program and not have an opinion? Remember, you're not asking for an ethereal truth scribed in stone—you just want an opinion, perception, or impression, and everyone has one. You know the saying about opinions right?

2. Whenever you can, try to keep your scaling to discrete answers (e.g., Yes or No) as opposed to the typical Likert-type scaling (e.g., strongly agree, agree, somewhat agree, etc.). For instance, if you ask the question, "Would you recommend this training?" and use the Yes/No options, you can report confidently and concisely:

- 90 percent of participants would recommend this training
  Alternatively, if you ask the same question using the "strongly agree" to "strongly disagree" continuum, you'll be stuck reporting a longer, blurrier response distribution like.
- 10 percent strongly agreed, 22 percent agreed, and 32 percent somewhat agreed with the following statement—"I would recommend this training."

Now which bullet would you rather include in your report?

3. Be specific with your response options. For instance, if you're asking participants to "[d]escribe the frequency of meetings you have with your leader to discuss your development plan," try not to give them options like "Very frequently" and "Less frequently." Just give them clear and specific response options like "Once a week," "Once a month," " Twice a year," and so on. This leaves far less room for subjective interpretation of the word "frequently" and relies solely on the number of actual meetings.

Table 1.1 Example of a Level 1 survey

Were you engaged by the subject and content of the training?	YES NO
If no, why not?	
Are you satisfied with the way the training was delivered?	YES NO
If no, why not?	
Are you satisfied with the facilitator?	YES NO
If no, why not?	
What was the best part of the experience?	
What was the worst part of the experience?	
Overall, are you satisfied with the training?	YES NO
Would you recommend this training to colleagues?	YES NO

See table 1.1 for an example of a full Level 1 survey with questions and scales

Gathering Your Level 1 Data and Creating Your Report

A simple hard copy survey handed out immediately after the training concludes will always work best. With all participants onsite and captive, it's easy to get a 100 percent response rate. If training is done online or via some other delivery mode, you should send an email with the Level 1 questions as soon as possible. I strongly recommend doing this the same day because your response rates will plunge dramatically as each day passes without follow-up.

When you get your responses back, you'll realize that your quick, practical, and concise approach to the questions and scales actually paid off. A few quick tallies of percentages (quantitative) and a quick content analysis of any open-text responses (qualitative) will conclude your Level 1 report. For your *quantitative* results, a quick snapshot of the discriminate items can be summed up in a single slide using a simple bar graph (see figure 1.1).

When it comes to reporting your *qualitative* results, just read through all your comments and start bucketing those responses that sound like they share a common theme. Identify your biggest

24 • Measuring and Maximizing Training Impact

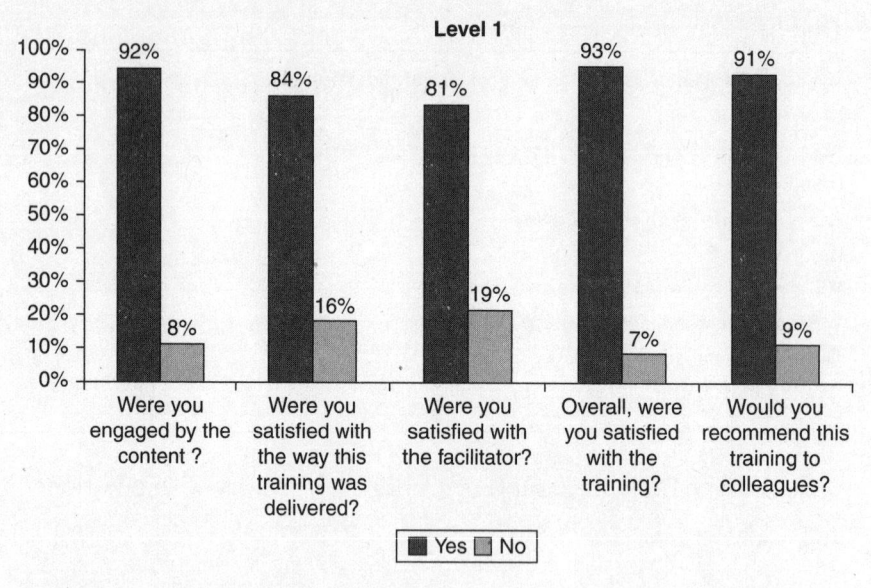

Level 1

Question	Yes	No
Were you engaged by the content?	92%	8%
Were you satisfied with the way this training was delivered?	84%	16%
Were you satisfied with the facilitator?	81%	19%
Overall, were you satisfied with the training?	93%	7%
Would you recommend this training to colleagues?	91%	9%

Figure 1.1 Quantitative results for Level 1.

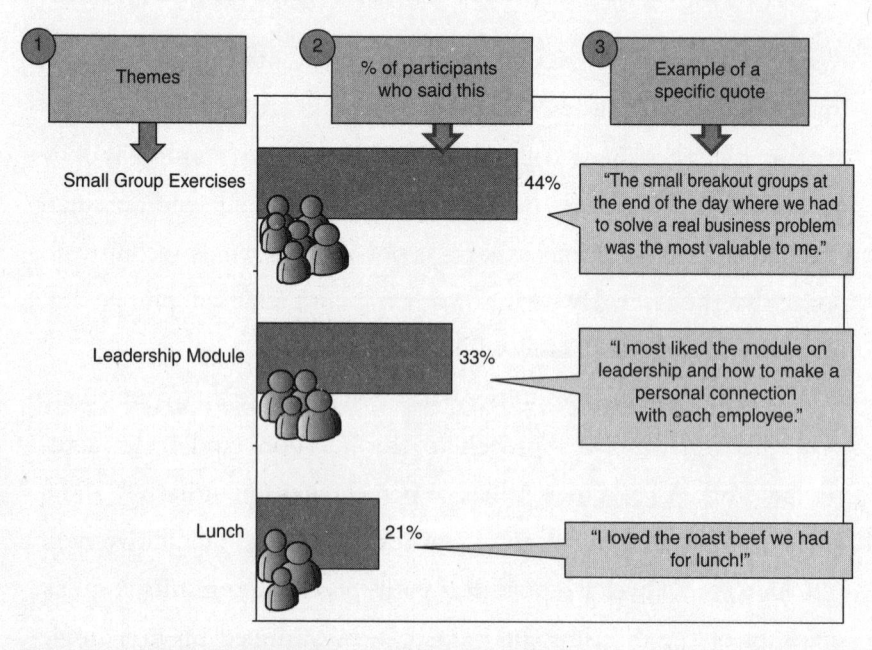

Themes	% of participants who said this	Example of a specific quote
Small Group Exercises	44%	"The small breakout groups at the end of the day where we had to solve a real business problem was the most valuable to me."
Leadership Module	33%	"I most liked the module on leadership and how to make a personal connection with each employee."
Lunch	21%	"I loved the roast beef we had for lunch!"

Figure 1.2 How to show qualitative results for Level 1.

themes, count up the percentage of responses that fell into each of those themes, and finally give a nice quote to exemplify the type of response that lives in that theme. See figure 1.2 highlighting the quick 1–2-3 steps.

This method for reporting qualitative data and summing up all open-ended responses is very popular with the business groups I work with, as it clearly and succinctly presents what could otherwise be pages and pages of participant input. Whether or not you go into this type of content analysis for each Level 1 question is of course up to you and your own organization, but I introduce it here because, as you will see in later chapters, this format becomes extremely valuable when summing up and reporting higher levels of evaluation. See figure 1.3 for the finished Level 1 slide.

Okay. Now that we've covered everything you'll need for a simple Level 1 (reaction and satisfaction with training), let's take a step forward to Level 2 and find out if anyone really learned anything.

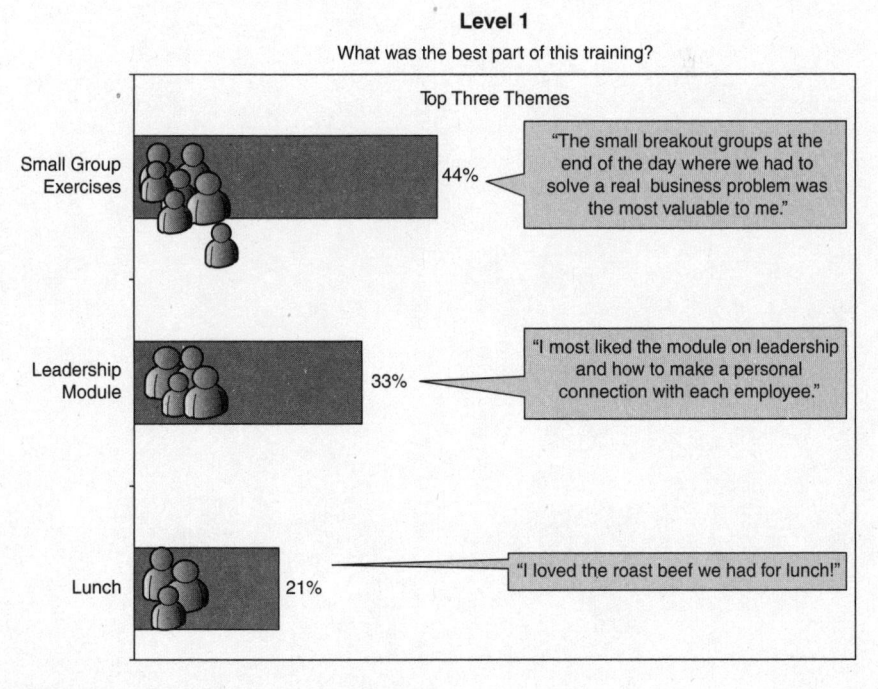

Level 1
What was the best part of this training?

Top Three Themes

- Small Group Exercises — 44% — "The small breakout groups at the end of the day where we had to solve a real business problem was the most valuable to me."
- Leadership Module — 33% — "I most liked the module on leadership and how to make a personal connection with each employee."
- Lunch — 21% — "I loved the roast beef we had for lunch!"

Figure 1.3 Sample of Level 1 qualitative report.

CHAPTER 2

Did They Learn Anything?

How to Collect, Analyze, and Report Level 2

Level 2 measures the amount of learning that occurred as a result of the training. That is, what new knowledge and skills were acquired from the training event? There are essentially two ways you can collect this information:

1. Pre- and post-test approach: measure an employee's knowledge/mastery before and after the training
2. Post-test approach: measure just once after training asking participant to report increase in knowledge and ability.

Pre- and Post-test Approach

The first approach is a pre-post design where you assess the employee's level of knowledge and/or skill before he/she attends the training (pre-test), then administer the same assessment after the training (post-test). You then calculate the difference between these two scores and the amount of that increase (from time 1 to time 2) becomes the measure of new knowledge and skills.

One fundamental problem with this approach is you will find yourself hoping and counting on most participants failing their pre-test miserably. After all, the lower the scores on these pre-tests, the more room for improvement as a result of your training, and the greater the potential difference on the post-test. Another huge problem is you have to administer the same assessment twice, which could be perceived (and rightly so) as a big waste of time. Most organizations already feel over-surveyed and have a very low tolerance for assessments that carelessly try to establish "baselines," especially if they don't point directly to clear, contingent, and actionable outcomes.

I've seen organizations put a lot of time and resources into developing this Level 2 pre-post design and it is not a pretty sight. Imagine asking employees and their leaders to take a long assessment only to tell them that they flunked it horribly. Although it may highlight initial knowledge gaps, it just won't make them feel good about you or your training. You don't want them to think you're trying to prove they're ignorant or incompetent right off the bat, do you? How receptive will they be to your training in the future? People in general are not motivated by someone highlighting what they don't know or how much they need to change from the way they have always done things. Overall, the pre-post design ends up being a very time-consuming, demotivating, and disengaging approach for participants.

Post-test Approach

A second, more practical, and far *easier* approach would be to skip the pre-test altogether and simply ask the employees a few targeted questions on a post-test. Here, you merely ask participants whether or not they learned something new and valuable as a result of training. Now you can capture the "difference" in knowledge before and after training and don't have to track and compare every single employee's pre- and post-test scores. Not only that, but now you have avoided insulting or demeaning your employees with a pre-test and have probably chopped down your data gathering and analysis time by about 75 percent.

Okay. Now you might ask—What about "knowledge assessments"? What about cases where we need to assign a hard numerical score to someone's knowledge because they need to achieve some minimum threshold of competence or compliance to return to their job after training? This might be the case with high-risk confidentiality practices, compliance training, and so on. Certainly, in these cases a more thorough test of knowledge is warranted, but this is technically not a Level 2 because it says nothing about the new knowledge gained from the training. That is, a pre-test was never administered so you still can't accurately assess what was learned in the training versus what the employee already knew. The bottom line is that these knowledge assessments (as they are typically called) and Level 2 scores are not the same thing. Although knowledge assessments are great to ensure everyone is at a certain level of knowledge, they still don't tell a story of knowledge acquired as a result of training.

At this stage of the evaluation, you don't have to do any rigorous analyses or complex correlations with other data sets. Keep it simple. Find out if they're smarter after the training and report it. Here are the only four items you really need to include in your short Level 2 survey, followed by a brief description of why I included each:

1. Did you gain new knowledge or skill from the training?
2. Was it important to your role?
3. Do you intend to apply and use it on the job?
4. What was your biggest takeaway? (open-ended)

1. Did you gain new knowledge or skill from the training?
   What you ultimately want to find out from any Level 2 is if there was an increase in knowledge or skills due to the training.

Instead of trying to calculate a difference score (post-test score minus pre-test score) for each participant, why not just ask participants outright if they learned anything? All we really want to do is establish that some important information was taught in training that has the *potential* to increase performance later on. If you end up with great behavior change and business results later in the study, you can then go back to these simple Level 2 scores and show that important new learning occurred (e.g., "93 percent of participants said they acquired valuable new knowledge and skills from this training"). Remember, Level 2 questions are just proving that employees learned something. How that learning affects their performance comes later. This is just the beginning of your ROI story. To take credit for business performance, you first have to show learning took place. Keep it simple.

2. Was it important to your role?

This question tells you a lot about the face validity and the potential impact on Level 3 (the number of on-the-job behaviors that can improve). Remember, we not only want to know that new knowledge or skills entered their brains, but we also want some assurance that this can be demonstrated frequently back on the job (the more often the better). We want to know that something we taught them will later manifest itself into consistent and *measurable* behavioral improvement. We can't say for sure at this point that they'll take the knowledge back to their everyday job, but at least if it's relevant and important to their role, we know they're more likely to. You can take all the glass blowing training you want, and you may graduate at the top of your class, but if you're a professional wrestler, it's of little importance and relevance to your role. I exaggerate, but you'd be surprised how many organizations just don't match the content to be learned with the roles they're supposed to improve. When these aren't aligned, the story of impact stops at Level 2. If they are aligned and knowledge changes critical on-the-job behaviors, you're already halfway across your bridge.

3. Do you intend to apply and use it on the job?

   As with the previous item, we can never say for sure whether shiny, brand new knowledge and skills will ever be used on the job, but one of the best predictors of application is the *intent* to apply. This simply speaks to the motivation of the participant. Will they wait for the opportunity to use their new skill or will they make the opportunity happen? If someone truly intends to buy another car in the next few months, chances are they'll soon roll up with some new wheels. If someone takes a few classes on healthy cooking, and intends on applying it their own kitchen, chances are they'll end up stocking their cupboards with a few healthier choices. If someone learns about ways they can increase the effectiveness of their presentations and intends to apply those techniques at their next speaking engagement, chances are they'll try them out. Will intentions always lead to actions? Heck no. But as with the previous item, it certainly says you're headed in the right direction. I don't ask this question because it powerfully predicts Level 3 results—I ask it because I want to build evidence that the employees learned something valuable and at the end of the day had all the best intentions to apply it.

4. What was your biggest takeaway? (open-ended)

   Here is where you collect the big qualitative quotes and testimonials to include in your Level 2 reporting. When they see that valuable new knowledge and skills were acquired (as evidenced by your previous questions), the first thing your audience will ask is: What types of new knowledge and skills? Here is where you add the color commentary to all your quantitative findings. Once they have some real-life examples in front of them, the percentage of people who actually said they learned something will be a lot more impressive. For example, a bullet saying "92 percent of employees learned something critical to their role" means a lot more when one example of that learning was "I've been struggling for weeks trying to create meaningful and motivational development plans with my direct reports and now I know exactly how to do it!" Now imagine 92 percent of your employees experiencing something similar. Quotes like this bring your numbers to life. Of course, don't count on all of them being so helpful for your impact story. In fact, one participant actually wrote, "My biggest piece of learning from this class was now I know I can't stay awake past 1:00 pm without any coffee."

See table 2.1 for a sample Level 2. And just like your Level 1, the results will be short and sweet. You'll again be reporting the response distribution for the Yes/No questions (quantitative) on one slide and the open-ended response summary (qualitative) on another (see figures 2.1 and 2.2).

Table 2.1 Sample Level 2 survey

Did you gain new knowledge and/or skills from this training?	YES	NO
If no, why not?		
Was the learning important to your role?	YES	NO
If no, why not?		
Do you intend to apply and use it on the job?	YES	NO
If no, why not?		
What was your one biggest takeaway from this training?		

Did They Learn Anything? • 33

Level 2

- Did you gain new knowledge/skills? Yes 84%, No 16%
- Is the learning important to your role? Yes 65%, No 35%
- Do you intend to apply and use it on the job? Yes 72%, No 28%

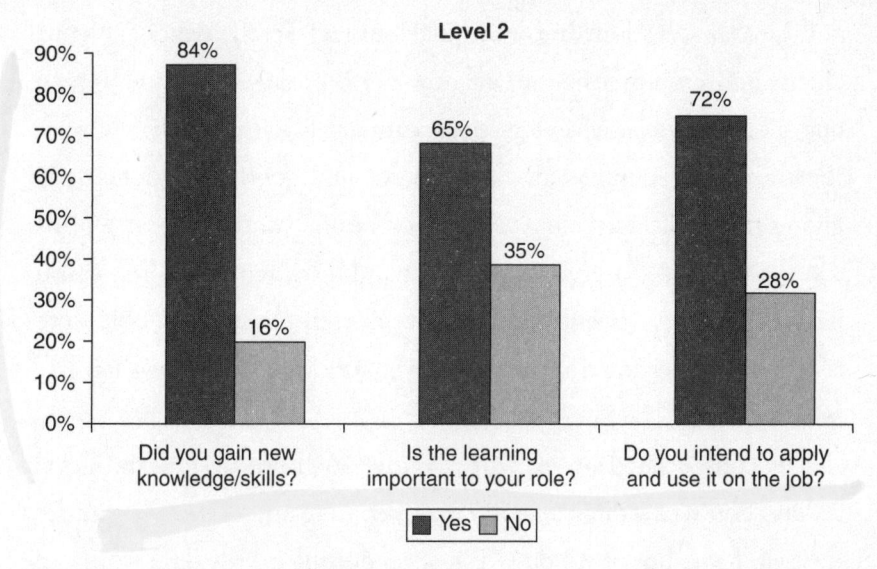

Figure 2.1 Quantitative results for Level 2.

Level 2
What was your biggest take-away?

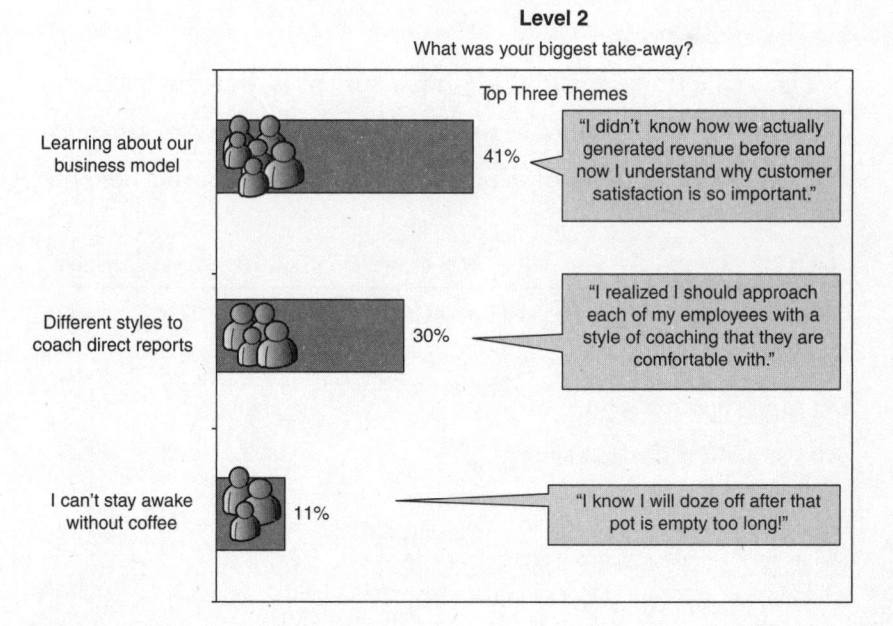

Top Three Themes

- Learning about our business model — 41% — "I didn't know how we actually generated revenue before and now I understand why customer satisfaction is so important."
- Different styles to coach direct reports — 30% — "I realized I should approach each of my employees with a style of coaching that they are comfortable with."
- I can't stay awake without coffee — 11% — "I know I will doze off after that pot is empty too long!"

Figure 2.2 Qualitative results for Level 2.

Combining Your Levels 1 and 2

When it comes to the administration of your Level 2 questions, here's another idea you might like. How about combining your Level 1 and Level 2 questions into *one* quick survey? To the delight of your clients and employees, you can now get both levels wrapped up in one short ten- to twelve-item questionnaire given immediately after the training is completed. Now you've just gone from potentially giving three different surveys (one for Level 1 and a pre- and post-test for Level 2) to giving just one combined version. What could have taken up to twenty minutes of your employees' valuable time is now chopped down to one simple survey that takes less than *five minutes*.

The consolidated survey will now give you both Level 1 and Level 2 data. You will still be able to create separate and consecutive slides for each level, but now you will just be pulling all the data you need from the same survey. See table 2.2 for an example of a combined Level 1 and Level 2.

The great thing about this simple survey is you can pick and choose which items you want to include in your report and also present various levels of detail depending on the interests and needs of

Table 2.2 Levels 1 and 2 measuring levels of satisfaction and learning from training

Were you engaged by the subject and content of the training?	YES	NO
If no, why not?		
Are you satisfied with the way the training was delivered?	YES	NO
If no, why not?		
Are you satisfied with the facilitator?	YES	NO
If no, why not?		
What was the best part of the experience?		
What was the worst part of the experience?		
Did you gain new knowledge and/or skills from this training?	YES	NO
If no, why not?		
What was your one biggest takeaway from this training?		
Was the learning important to your role?	YES	NO
If no, why not?		
Do you intend to apply and use it on the job?	YES	NO
Overall, are you satisfied with the training?	YES	NO
Would you recommend this training to colleagues?	YES	NO
Any other comments?		

your audience. For instance, if you are presenting the results back to your training group or your HR colleagues, you may want to include more or all of the qualitative analyses (e.g., comments on the best and worst part of the training, biggest learning takeaway, etc.). Since they can make changes to content and potentially improve the delivery of training, they will consider this detailed information very valuable.

On the other hand, you may have an audience of business leaders who only want the highest level synopsis for each evaluation level. Here, you'll find yourself having to shelf many of your original Level 1 and Level 2 charts, graphs, and analyses (especially the comment and content analysis) and replacing them with an extremely abridged, quick, and dirty version of your results. In fact, if you are creating an evaluation dashboard or just an overall summary slide, you'll have to capture all of the participants' satisfaction and learning in only two bullet points. If you find yourself forced to squeeze all your great Level 1 and Level 2 findings down to a couple of soundbites, you should hone in on two specific questions from the survey:

Level 1: Overall are you satisfied with the training experience?
Level 2: Did you gain new knowledge and skills from your training?

Using the responses from these two questions you will be able to quickly quantify and represent your Levels 1 and 2 with a quick snapshot (see figure 2.3).

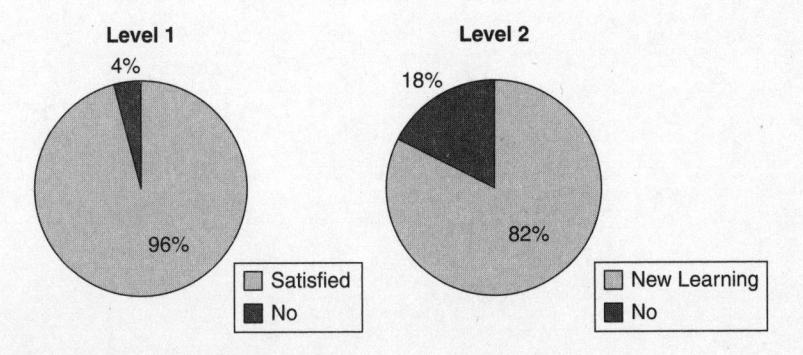

Figure 2.3 Overall snapshot report for Levels 1 and 2.

Remember, as your evaluation story evolves and you report higher levels of impact (e.g., behavior change and business improvements), the value and significance of these earlier levels will greatly diminish. Your methods will become more sophisticated and your data will be more robust, so Levels 1 and 2 will naturally become a very small component of a far more comprehensive evaluation story.

Okay. Speaking of evolving our story, let's take the next step on our journey and jump right into Level 3, Behavior Change. Are your employees really doing anything different?

CHAPTER 3

Are They Doing Anything Different?

How to Collect, Analyze, and Report Level 3

Level 3 describes the amount of actual *observable* behavior change demonstrated by employees as a result of training. That is, what are employees doing differently (and hopefully better) in the months after the formal training event ends? You can measure post-training behavior anywhere from a day to a year after training, but I recommend *3 months* because it's short enough to still be fresh and long enough to give trainees time to demonstrate some level of sustained improvement. At this three-month period, you will ask participants and coworkers to assess very specific and observable behaviors. By the end of this chapter you'll know exactly which behaviors to choose for your assessment, but for now, remember these two simple rules:

1. The behavior must be visible to coworkers
2. The behavior must be valuable to the business

You would be astonished if I told you how many flagrant violations of these two simple rules are out there clogging up and polluting otherwise decent Level 3 evaluations. The behaviors you need to identify and the data you will need to quantify those behaviors will practically fall right into your lap if you design the right approach and the right questions up front. While there are several different ways to design your evaluation and collect your Level 3 data, in this chapter I'm going to show you the very best way.

Choose Your Design

Do You Need to Measure before and after Training?

Okay. You might be saying to yourself right now—we took some great shortcuts for collecting our Level 2 data, but surely for a Level 3 analysis we'll need to develop an elaborate pre-post research design to compare a baseline "point of departure" to some post-intervention "point of arrival"—right? Wrong. The pre-post research methodology sounds very impressive and scientific (and it is in many situations), but in fact, a pre-post design at this level of evaluation, in a real work setting, may prove even more problematic than at your Level 2.

Adopting the traditional notion that measuring behavior change must involve an exhaustive (and exhausting) collection of baseline data to then compare to post-training data is what I see as the single biggest obstacle to getting robust Level 3 data and results. It is the biggest reason why less than 15 percent of all organizations will even attempt to reach a Level 3 evaluation. Training groups attempting to collect all these data and measure training effectiveness in this way are in fact making it much more difficult, tedious, and cumbersome than it has to be. There is a far more practical, concise, and quicker way to achieve these Level 3 results. That's right—you guessed it—simply cut out the pretest and baseline data altogether. And beyond making your life a lot easier and asking a lot less time from the business for survey-taking, the most important win of all is you will actually end up with a more reliable and meaningful report that your business clients will truly appreciate.

Don't get too excited though because I will return to some pre and post data collection for Level 4 and I certainly don't want you to discount its effectiveness and impact. For many researchers in many different scenarios, the pre-post design is in fact a great way to measure the change or improvement caused by a particular type of treatment or intervention. For instance, if you are a medical doctor or researcher, you definitely want to get a baseline on someone's weight, blood pressure, hormone levels, and so on before your treatment program begins and then take the very same measurements again right after. Similarly, if you are comparing hard measures of productivity and business metrics in an organization (Level 4), your pre- and post-training comparisons may become absolutely critical. However, for a Level 3, relying on this approach can lead to horribly inaccurate results and even worse conclusions.

No Room for Improvement

So, why does the pre-post design work so well in some scenarios, but not for measuring Level 3 behavior change in employees? The answer is simple—it all has to do with the "*room*" you have for improvement. More specifically, the room any employee has for measured improvement will depend on the behaviors you choose to measure, the scale you use to measure, and the bias of your responses. Allow me to explain.

What we ultimately want to get from a pre-post design calculation is a "difference score" (postscore minus prescore). If you are working in the medical field and you are measuring things like weight loss or blood pressure, your measure before the intervention may be 296 pounds and your measure afterwards may be 209 pounds. Your difference score here would be a very reliable and valid 87 pounds. Notice that for this scenario, using this scale, there is tremendous variability in the potential scoring and the units of measure are truly objective. That is, people going through the weight-loss training program could have feasibly lost 2 pounds or 200 pounds. This spacious room for improvement and the nonbias recording of a weight scale is what makes the pre-post design an excellent option in this situation.

In organizational settings however, measuring a behavior at time 1 (pre) and then again at time 2 (post) is vastly more ambiguous and grossly more subjective. Unless you are counting some very specific and distinct behavioral units (e.g., number of meetings held, amount of times someone shows up late, number of times a speaker says "umm" during his presentations, etc.) under some very controlled conditions, trying to get a true and reliable measure at either time will be challenging at best. Then, to take those two potentially inaccurate measures and try to calculate a true difference score will be next to impossible. Unfortunately, the concrete units of measure and the tightly controlled conditions that should be there for a good pre-post design are extremely rare when it comes to measuring behavior in the workplace. Therefore, what we are often left with, in almost all work contexts, are situations where we mean well and want to impose a good pre-post design, but the employee behaviors we measure are ill-defined, the scales we use are insensitive, and the raters we use are biased.

For instance, an incredibly popular method for measuring training effectiveness in many organizations is using a multirater survey or a 360-degree feedback tool. This is administered once before the training and then again several months after the training. The two scores are then compared in an attempt to quantify training "effectiveness." This is an absolutely horrible mistake. Why "absolutely horrible" you ask? Well, let's consider a typical behavioral/competency assessment. What does it look like? For most assessments, you will find an inventory of long-winded, ill-defined behaviors, which you are supposed to rate using an equally ill-defined set of options. You will have six or seven options (at best) to choose from on your pre-test (e.g., "extremely ineffective" to "extremely effective") and then the same scale on the post-test:

PRE...

Rate this employee's ability to...

Extremely ineffective	Ineffective	Somewhat ineffective	Somewhat effective	Effective	Extremely effective
1	2	3	4	5	6

POST...

Rate this employee's ability to...

Extremely ineffective	Ineffective	Somewhat ineffective	Somewhat effective	Effective	Extremely effective
1	2	3	4	5	6

So right off the bat, we have two scores or ratings of "effectiveness" that are completely subjective and may even be rated by a few different employees at time 1 and time 2 (i.e., a participant's leader and/or coworkers may change over the course of several months). Now our next step is to take those two inaccurate scores, compare them, and calculate a difference score. And this one score is supposed to define all our behavior change and training effectiveness. Is this not a problem? No wonder we have such a hard time convincing our business that training is beneficial.

First off, for the assessment to be a sensitive one, there should be considerable variability in possible scores at time 1 and then again at time 2. In the scales given earlier, from a possibility perspective, you can only score a 1–6 on your pretest and only a possible 1–6 on your post-test. Hence, the biggest possible improvement or difference score you can have is 5. And that is the best possible and most improbable scenario! In actual organizational settings, raters are usually very lenient when rating other employees' competencies or behaviors so you will find both the pre and the post scores skewed (probably 80 percent of all responses) to the high end of the scale. That is, when employees are asked to rate themselves or coworkers, most will rate even the worst of coworkers or leaders with some less harmful mid-scale value. This very real and prevalent attenuation of responses means the difference scores that are supposed to define all of your wonderful training impact are now limited to only one or two incremental points.

Now imagine you have a whole bunch of trainees going through your program to "improve" one of their leadership competencies. Also imagine the vast majority of them have already scored a 4 or a 5 (e.g., "somewhat effective" or "effective") on the pre-test. This means no matter how great your program is, they can at best move from a 4 or a 5 to a 6. Are you going to tell your clients and stakeholders that they spent $10 million on training, and you spent over a year collecting pre-post data, just to show them their employees moved from a 5 to a 6? Or, as a large group they moved from an average (mean) of 4.2 to 4.9? Good luck with that presentation! The point is, without more sensitive measures and greater variability in scores, you really can't capture the true levels of improvement that actually occurred. And you'll leave your business partners scratching their heads wondering how this incredibly small behavior change was worth their huge investment. You literally left them *no room for improvement.*

How Horrible Can It Get?

As we just saw, an ill-fated pre-post design can mean a horrible underestimation of your training's true effectiveness. But it can literally get worse. Sometimes, a pre-post design can not only restrict and leave little or no room for employees to get "better," but can actually lead to the conclusion that training made everyone worse! I call this the "ignorance is bias" effect. If you've heard of the saying "ignorance is bliss," it implies that in some situations, not being fully aware of certain things can actually be a good thing. For instance, you might think you're a great singer and continue to fantasize about the day you can trade in your business slacks for a diamond-studded jumpsuit. If however, one day you did audition among true talents, you might come to the dismal realization that your dream is absolutely over and you should never quit your day job. Okay, enough about me—let me get back to my point. In this case, your ignorance (before the audition) might be bliss, but it's certainly not a fair assessment of your ability. Even if it was not deliberate, your ignorance is indeed biased.

When it comes to pre-post competency assessments in organization, this lack of knowledge and awareness can devastate your Level 3 results. For instance, employees have a tendency to think they know more or are better at something than they really are. Then of course after taking some in-depth training and gaining new skills in a particular area, they realize they were relatively bad to begin with. Similarly, they might think a coworker really knows what he's doing, then after spending several months with him and increasing their own skills, they realize just how incompetent he really is. What these two scenarios mean in terms of pre-post scoring is that your pre-test will be inflated while your post-test will be a more conservative and true estimate of ability. This not only dilutes your results regarding the true level of training impact, but can actually make the impact appear negative. How about this headline: "Our training made employees less effective." Good luck with that presentation.

Okay. Still want to use a pre-test and a post-test to measure your training effectiveness? Not convinced yet? Here's one final example: Imagine a cooking school wants to measure how effective their new training program is. As a participant, they decide to give you a self-report preassessment. You're already well known for your famous French toast, you're an absolute star at Thanksgiving dinner every year, and your friends can't stop raving about your homemade brownies (or Super Bowl wings for men who don't bake brownies). When given the question "How would you rate your current cooking ability?" you decide you're "very good" and make your selection:

How would you rate your current cooking ability?

Terrible	Weak	Not too good	Good	Very good	Exceptional
1	2	3	4	(5)	6

A few days later you begin going through this fairly advanced cooking course where you learn about the perfect risotto, a cantaloupe-infused reduction sauce, and a balsamic and lemon painted bass with grapefruit and mango adornments. You also learn about which wines come from where and which years make for the perfect match with your seared salmon on a bed of garlic-spinach leaves. To make a long story short, it's now three months after your training program and you're shopping for spices and ingredients you never knew existed.

Now what happens when you receive the same assessment again and you are asked, "How would you rate your cooking ability?" With your humbling exposure to fine cuisine, hours of watching culinary masters dice in a blur, and your overall new appreciation of cooking, what would you rate yourself? Let's assume you give yourself a more grounded "Good" this time around:

How would you rate your current cooking ability?

Terrible	Weak	Not too good	Good	Very good	Exceptional
1	2	3	(4)	5	6

You hand in your ratings and off you go. Now the poor slob measuring training effectiveness compares your prescore and your postscore. Congratulations—you've just spent months in cooking class and you actually got worse. And what should the poor evaluation guy report to your sponsors who might have paid for the training? What kind of ROI do you think you'd end up with for this cooking class? Was this course really a flop? Absolutely not—you jumped to a whole new level of cooking, had incredible improvement, and experienced tremendous growth as a wannabe chef. The problem was it couldn't be captured with this evaluation. While this seems like a somewhat exaggerated example, these types of faulty methods are being applied in organizations everywhere (including yours). The cumulative and end result of all these "little" evaluation missteps is that powerful training all over the world never gets its recognition. And training within your own organizations continues a desperate and often futile struggle to prove its worth.

Make Room for Improvement: Just Use a Post-test

Now think of the training examples given so far and imagine the participants never got a pre-test at all, and simply got one post-test three months after training was completed. And on this post-test, they find an "improvement" scale. Here, the raters are given a short list of key behaviors or skills that should have improved as a result of the training, and simply asked to identify the level or amount of improvement they observed during the three months after the training occurred. Now, instead of relying on the "difference" between two disparate scores that may lack reliability and validity from time 1 and time 2 (pre-post design), you are directly asking raters to quantify that difference. The options the raters have to choose from can begin with "exceptional improvement" and end with "no improvement" or even "got worse." For example, if one of the primary objectives of the training was to make an employee deliver better presentations, the self, leader, and/or coworkers would be asked:

How much improvement (if any) have you observed in this person's presentation skills over the last three months?

Got worse	No improvement	Little improvement	Some improvement	Significant improvement	Exceptional improvement
1	2	3	4	5	6

If you think about it, this method, with your new improvement scale is actually allowing you to identify and capture the "difference score" that you were ultimately looking for in the first place *and* it's getting it done in a more effective, practical, and valid way because you are completely eradicating the problems and biases that arise using the pre-test. There is now more room built into your scale to capture varying levels of actual improvement and you've also guarded against the "ignorance" bias. Not only that, but you no longer have to track each employee over the post-training period to match and compare individual prescores to postscores. That alone cuts your data collection and analysis work by more than half. You now have one simple survey administered three months after the training event and it captures all the data you need for your Level 3. And the biggest win goes to the business because you only have to survey your audience once.

What you've created with this new approach is a simple, practical, and just plain better way to capture exactly what you want: A true and valid reflection of improvement not diluted by an oblivious prescore, and a set of responses with much greater variability. Additionally, you now have a number value (level of improvement) for Level 3 that you can correlate to any other variable or construct you might be interested in measuring (e.g., do employees who score high on improvement also score higher on other questions about their immediate work environment?). This range of Level 3 scores is essential for building a solid Level 4 and 5, and becomes absolutely crucial for measuring Level 6 as I'll show you in later chapters. Okay. Let's start building your post-training Level 3 assessment.

Choose Your Behaviors

So now you've chosen your research design, and you know you'll be using an improvement scale on the post-training assessment, but what about the actual behaviors you are going to ask about? What are the specific Level 3 behaviors you should be targeting in your evaluation?

This should be easy—right? Whether developed internally or externally, whoever brought a training solution to your organization and convinced the higher-ups to spend thousands of dollars must have had a sound business case—right? And in that business case, they would have identified which key behaviors the training would change—right? And of course, also included in that comprehensive business case would be a proposal about how those behaviors would improve the business—right? I mean, surely someone at some point proposed that training would teach something (Level 2) that would lead to improved behavior (Level 3) that in turn would improve some business metric (Level 4). And these fundamental steps or linkages have to be documented somewhere—right? All you need to do is get your hands on this fantastic business case and there staring back at you will be all the Level 3 behaviors you need for your survey—right?

Wrong. Unfortunately, a vast majority of organizations develop and roll out their training first, and then scramble to make a business case for that training later. Sure, they may do some work up front to identify their performance gaps and perhaps call out some overarching competencies they need to improve, but for some bizarre reason they don't get into the very necessary business of detailing and proposing the specific cause-and-effect linkages between their desired results and the employee behaviors that will lead to those results. Training changes behaviors and behaviors change business results. *These are the most fundamental links that hold your "bridge" together.* If you remember figure I.1 in the Introduction, "The Bridge" is actually made up of all the levels of evaluation extending from the training event to the desired business outcomes. It's no coincidence that your Level 3 is right smack in the middle of this precarious path between the training and the bottom-line payoff. If you think of any bridge and where you are most vulnerable when crossing, it's the midpoint. You are the furthest from your departure site and also from your destination. This is the last place you want to find faults or hear any crackling under your feet. If the bridge's connection isn't solid and fortified here at the pivotal and critical midpoint, your whole path starts to crumble and you'll eventually plummet into the vast sea of wasted training programs. The nexus that truly connects any learning to effectiveness is this Level 3 employee behavior.

Make Your Business Case

In a perfect world, training content creators and training evaluators would be very deliberately partnering up front to create and align the business case with the evaluation strategy. Remember, the evaluation of all training should be simply testing whether the cause-and-effect relationships proposed within the original business case are in fact happening. Unfortunately, this type of synergy and *business casing* doesn't happen up front and the burden of showing the "value" of any given training program falls squarely and solely on the shoulders of the evaluator *after* the training is developed, purchased, and rolled out. Instead of asking, "Can you tell us if our business case is working the way we planned?" someone will dump the final training product in your lap and ask, "Does this training work?" This means it's up to you to define the causes and effects. This means it's up to you as the training evaluator to identify what behaviors changed (Level 3) and how they impacted the business (Level 4). This means it's up to you to build your own bridge.

I refer to this process of defining your business case and creating these important linkages as the simple *ROI* of building your bridge. As I mentioned in my introduction, training architects should always begin this process by clearly defining the bottom-line business results they want (the destination) and then working their way backwards. Once you define the desired results and the metrics that are supposed to improve as a result of your training, you can then (and only then) identify the employee behaviors that will get you there. And finally you can look at all those behaviors and see which ones you can really bring to life with training. See figure 3.1 for the fundamental linkages that make your business case and connect your bridge.

R—What are the *results* you want from training? What metrics are important to the business? These are the daily, weekly, monthly, or quarterly numbers that businesses rigorously track to define their performance and profitability. The better you identify these desired outcome measures, the stronger and more valuable you can make your business case.

The ROI of Building Your Bridge Backwards
Creating Your Business Case

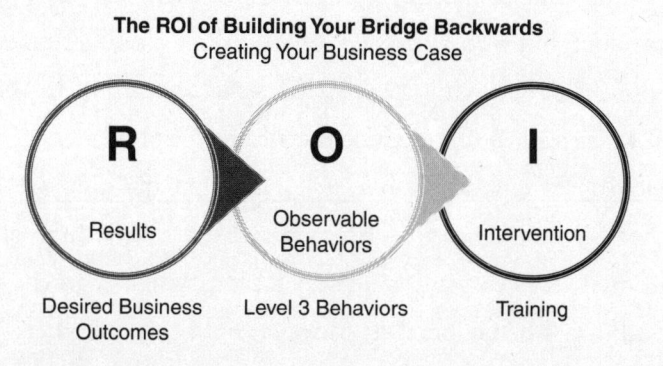

R — Results — Desired Business Outcomes
O — Observable Behaviors — Level 3 Behaviors
I — Intervention — Training

Figure 3.1 The ROI of building your bridge (the business case).

O—What are the *observable behaviors* that will get you there? What do employees need to do differently and/or better on the job to directly impact these critical metrics? These are the demonstrable behaviors that separate strong performers from weak ones and need to become a bigger part of every employee's daily routine.

I—What are the key pieces of the learning *initiative* that will lead to those behaviors? What new knowledge and skills do you really need to teach employees during the training experience? These are the critical objectives that dictate the training content. The more training architects and content developers know about the goals, results, and behaviors they are supposed to improve, the more powerful and effective they can be at creating (or buying) the content that really drives the business.

I'll share a quick example of how this worked for a customer-facing sales organization:

> Starting with *results*—The first thing we did was form a small team of allies deep within the business. This included two key stakeholders, two customer-facing employees that lived and breathed the sales metrics every day, as well as one analyst that used these metrics to forecast things like profitability and growth for each particular group and region. We quickly found that the real money-maker metrics were not the straight sales of a particular product, but rather the sales of long-term services that support the products. Knowing these metrics mattered most to the business, we agreed to target these metrics for improvement.
>
> Moving to *observable behaviors*, the next question we had to ask was—what employee behaviors drove the selling of those additional services? And were they a bit different than the typical or traditional behaviors that drove straight product sales. Which on-the-job behaviors did employees need to improve to sell more long-term services and hit those higher revenue targets? What

we found from this exploration was that the highest performers (greatest revenue-generators) had a few behaviors that really distinguished them from their average performing coworkers. For example, one distinguishing behavior (that everyone observed) was the more successful sales specialists created a quick rapport and asked the customer significantly more questions about their long-term needs. Another behavior was using significantly more humor in their repertoire.

Identifying these behaviors as high predictors of success, we then decided on the overarching objectives of the training program, which ended up being fairly different than some of the traditional sales programs that were available off the shelf. This was how we identified the employee knowledge and skills that needed to be covered and taught in the content. This is how we started creating (or shopping for) our *initiative*.

Of course, once we built these connections and got true buy-in from our business leaders, the whole evaluation process after training was incredibly streamlined and simple. By starting the conversation with results and building this blueprint of our bridge backwards, we were then able to build a stronger and more powerful bridge forward. As I'll demonstrate later, making these strong linkages not only helps you to measure and report the effects of training, but actually maximizes those effects and increases training's ROI. And remember, the most critical and pivotal link in this bridge, whether you are building backward or forward, is your Level 3.

No Good Business Case? No Fear—All Is Not Lost

Okay. So we don't live in a perfect world, you didn't get all this R-O-I business casing done up front, and you can't dig up an old archived business proposal because no one bothered to create one. Now your chief learning officer just walked into your office and asked you to show some of the C-levels, and some other stakeholders, how the training they already rolled out is "working." Well, now it's up to you to tell the impact story and define the employee *behaviors* that link the training to the business outcomes. So you've got a little work to do, but I'll help you find just the right Level 3 behaviors to measure and include in your evaluation. The very first thing you'll need to do is get out your machete and goggles and *cut through all the crap.*

Cut through All the Crap

Training content, especially off the shelf, is purposefully broad and generic so that it appeals to a wide range of very diverse organizational needs. Vendors (and we can't blame them) obviously want their products to be relevant for as many client organizations and audiences as possible. Consequently, a vast majority of training solutions seek to and purport to improve a very large pool of employee behaviors. However, there will only be a few very specific behaviors that will truly be affected by the overall training experience and of those, there will be even fewer that matter to your business. Therefore it becomes your job, as the evaluator of training within your unique business, to identify and evaluate only those choice behaviors that will be most impacted, that are readily observable, and at the same time are the biggest drivers of employee productivity and business performance. It is this *intersection* (see figure 3.2) that ultimately defines the domain of your Level 3 behaviors. To make it to the very small sweet spot in the center, each Level 3 behavior has to be:

- impacted by the training content;
- measurable/observable to others;
- critical to the business.

Which Behaviors Do You Evaluate?

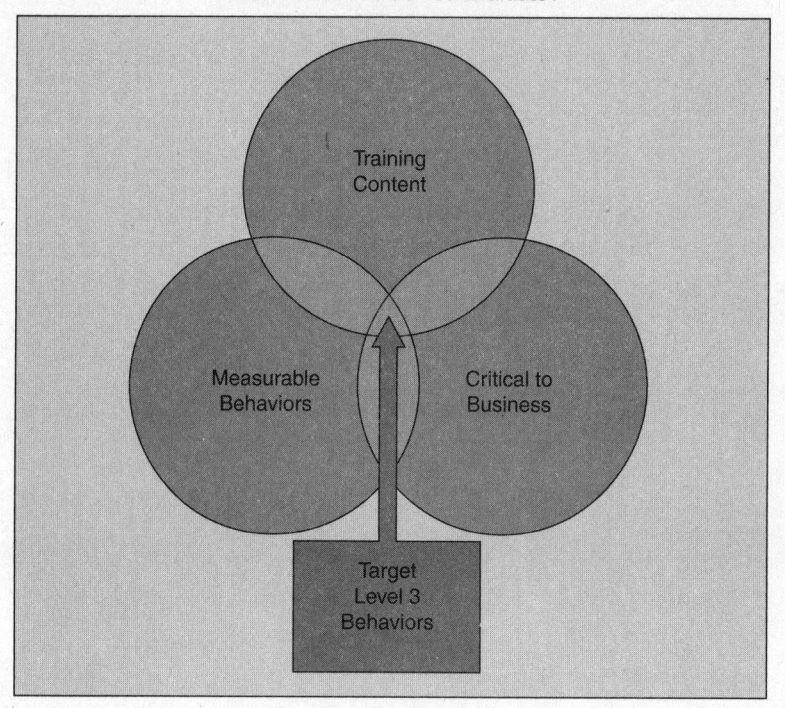

[Venn diagram with three overlapping circles labeled "Training Content", "Measurable Behaviors", and "Critical to Business", with an arrow pointing from a box labeled "Target Level 3 Behaviors" to the center intersection]

Figure 3.2 Domain of Level 3 behaviors.

As you can clearly see from the bubbles in figure 3.2, the vast majorities of organizational behaviors are either measurable/observable, but not critical to the business, or are critical to the business, but not readily measurable. Or, if you do know behaviors that are both measurable and critical to the business, you can't find them properly addressed and targeted by the training. Just to give you an example, I've populated figure 3.3 with some behaviors that I found within each bubble when I was evaluating a leadership training program for a large financial company. Here, you can see that although many behaviors are pulled into the mix, only a few will meet the criteria for all three bubbles and really hit that center sweet spot.

As you can see from this example, Delivering Great Presentations is very readily observable and measurable, but not a direct driver of

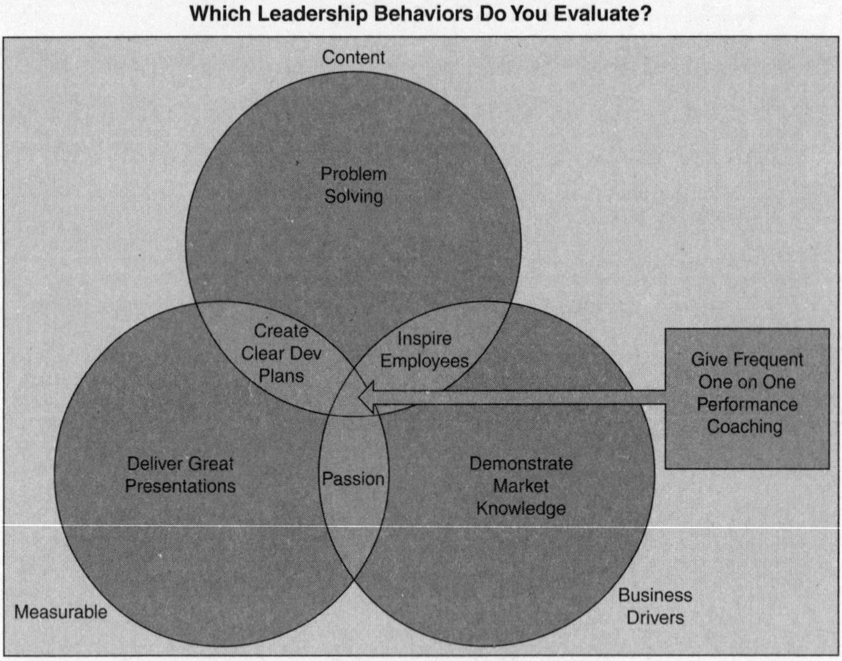

Which Leadership Behaviors Do You Evaluate?

[Venn diagram with three overlapping circles labeled Content, Measurable, and Business Drivers. Content circle contains "Problem Solving". Measurable circle contains "Deliver Great Presentations". Business Drivers circle contains "Demonstrate Market Knowledge". Overlaps contain "Create Clear Dev Plans", "Inspire Employees", and "Passion". An arrow points to the center from a box labeled "Give Frequent One on One Performance Coaching".]

Figure 3.3 Picking the right leadership behaviors for a Level 3.

the business. Similarly, showing great expertise in one's particular business market (Demonstrating Market Knowledge) is a huge predictor of productivity, but is hard to observe and measure by others right after training. And finally, while something like Passion can be observed, and is of course an incredible business driver, it's hard to find a training program that could teach and instantly "improve" it. You can also see that the only behavior that shows up in all three bubbles is "Give Frequent One on One Performance Coaching" because it is part of the training content that is readily observable, measurable, and known to drive the business. Of course by the end of your own analysis, for your particular training program, you will have more than one behavior in the center. The point is, using these criteria will help you narrow down the many possible employee behaviors to a mighty few. In other words, it'll help you cut through all the crap.

Okay, so we know *what* we want, now all we need to know is *how* to get there. What does the actual process look like? How do we take any current training program or experience, get rid of all the irrelevant stuff, and pull out just a few core behaviors to plug into our Level 3 assessment?

How to "Cut the Crap"

This whole process of honing in on the most valuable behaviors should work like a simple filter or purifier. At the very top, you can dump in just about everything. The majority of crap gets trapped on the top screen, while the clearer, purer stuff makes its way down to the next level. At this next level, even more impurities get caught, leaving only the clearest, purest stuff at the bottom. In the very same way, we start out with all this training content being dumped in at the top. At the very first level, we need to screen all of the so-called trainable behaviors to make sure they are readily observable and measurable. These observable behaviors then make it down to the second level where we screen them again to make sure they impact the business. It is through this two-stage cutting or purifying process that whatever we have left becomes our list of viable Level 3 behaviors. Figure 3.4 depicts the process.

Your First Cut: Identify Your Most Observable Behaviors

The first thing you should do is attend the training. *And don't take any notes.* I say this because I want you to get completely immersed in the participant experience and forget you're an evaluator. You are there to learn. A few days after completing the training, go back and review the training content (modules, materials, etc.) highlighting all the training *objectives*. Here, you might want to simply flip to the beginning or end of the training materials where there should be a

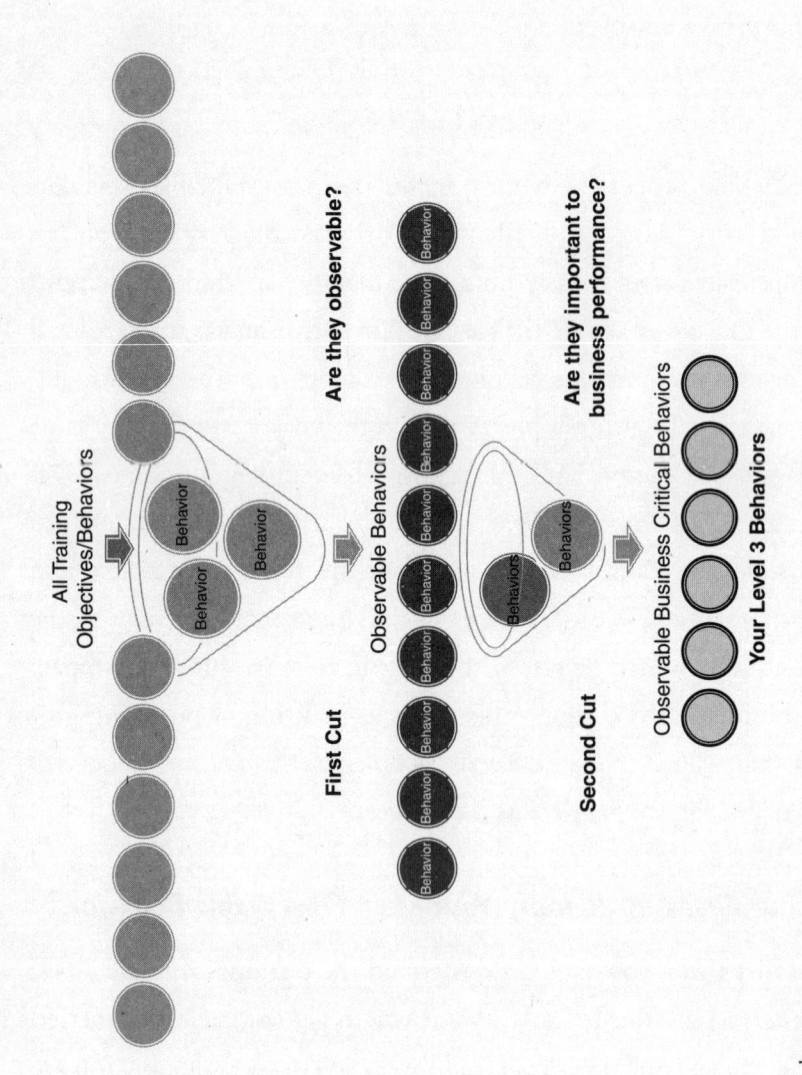

Figure 3.4 Cutting the crap.

list of a few core learning objectives (e.g., "By the end of this module/training you should be able to..."). Look for these big bolded bullets and create a list. Next, go down this list, item by item, and think about your training experience. With this lens, get rid of all the fluff (long-winded corporate jargon and psycho-babble) and rewrite the behaviors in common simple words. Here, by all means, don't be afraid to break one bullet or objective down into two or three separate and smaller behaviors. Each of your behaviors should stand alone. Be simple and concise. And finally, hone in on only those behaviors that are directly observable and truly expected to change over the next three month after training. What should each employee be doing *differently* after this particular training? What should each employee be doing *more* of after this training? What should each employee be doing *better* after this training? And remember; make sure each of these promised and predicted outcomes is observable. If they improve in the next few months, you should see it. If you can't see it, you can't measure it!

I can't tell you how many Level 3 surveys I've seen across all types of organizations that include so-called behaviors like Critical Thinking, where the rater or assessor is asked to: "Rate this employee's ability to think critically." What? How would I be able to tell what's really going on in another person's head? Heck—how would the participant (who owns the head) even know how to rate that? What would be the cues and telltale signs that this person got incrementally better over the next three months after training? Anyway, beware—while some training might say it will improve a competency like "Critical Thinking," it is up to you as the evaluation expert to either dump it altogether from your list, or try to break it down to a few tangible, observable indicators. Whatever criteria and behaviors you choose, you should conclude this part of your "crap-cutting" with a list of about *10–12 of your most measurable behaviors.*

Your Second Cut: Identify Your Biggest Business Drivers

Your second stage of this filtering process is to take your new list of 10–12 measurable behaviors and hone it down even further to just those that truly and most directly impact the business. Which ones will lead to the most important business outcomes? Here, you should go directly to your business leaders and partners, bring your list, lay it down in front of them, and just ask them. In this meeting, there are a couple of key things you should probe for.

First, what are the metrics they track on a weekly and monthly basis? What's important to them? What do they use to measure their performance and report their own business health as an organization? What are the metrics that analysts and stakeholders look for to define profitability and growth? How might the behaviors you put in front of them help them improve those results?

Second, what are their new goals as an organization? What do they really want to achieve by the end of the year? Do they want to penetrate a new market or change the perception of their brand? What changes do they plan on implementing? What current initiatives are important to them? And again, how might the behaviors you put in front of them help their employees get there? For example, if a company feels it needs to put more focus on creating exceptional customer service, the behaviors they choose at this level will be those that relate directly to creating happy customers. This might mean behaviors like "resolving customer issues" and "probing to identify customer needs" move to the forefront.

And finally, what employee behaviors and competencies will help them stay competitive in the future? Are they trying to build pipelines and career paths? Have they profiled what their future leaders look like? Which of the behaviors you listed can help them build this future capability? If a company knows that the only way to stay competitive in the future is to build a strong bench of innovation and creativity, they should look for those behavioral indicators when selecting their final Level 3 behaviors.

As I mentioned earlier in this chapter, training content will always be far too broad for you to measure everything with your Level 3. This means it's ultimately up to the evaluator and the stakeholders to nail down the specific behaviors that are most important to the business at the time. When you're done asking all your questions and you've chopped down your list based on these business impact criteria, you should be left with only *six–eight of the most measurable, business-critical behaviors for your Level 3*.

The best part about this meeting with the business is you are not only honing in on your critical Level 3 behaviors, but also laying all the groundwork for your Level 4. Remember, for your overall evaluation story to make sense, your Level 3 needs to be inextricably linked to your Level 4. That is, in order for you to truly *isolate* the effects of training, you need to show that your Level 3 behaviors *cause* your Level 4 business improvements. While the best scenario would have been to identify and get buy-in on all these linkages up front (before the training was even launched), it's still not too late to collect all the data you need to create those causal paths and tell a comprehensive story of impact. In fact, chances are most of your evaluation requests will come during this postlaunch period, so you'll often have to make all these linkages without that perfect, archived business case in front of you. It'll ultimately be up to you to choose the right Level 3 behaviors and if you don't get them right, *your bridge will simply fall apart*.

Using Competency Models to Build Your Level 3 Questions

Another good resource to help you "cut the crap" and get at the behaviors and business drivers that really matter is a competency model. A competency model is essentially a list of employee competencies and behaviors that have already been identified as being critical to someone's success in a particular role or job function. This "profile" describes all the important characteristics and skills the ideal employee brings to the table. In terms of process, after you attend the training and review all the objectives from your training initiative, simply compare them to the behaviors in the competency model. Is there any overlap? There definitely should be. Do any of the training objectives map directly and almost verbatim to the behavioral indicators in the model? While competency models can include over 50 behaviors, you're looking for only a targeted few of the most powerful descriptors that relate directly back to your training experience. For instance, one organization-wide leadership competency model included eight overarching competencies and eight behavioral indicators under each of those competencies. That left me with a total of 64 behavioral indicators to sort through. After reviewing all the core lessons and objectives of a particular piece of leadership training, I ended up plucking out only 8 and using them (almost verbatim) for my Level 3 questions.

Although varying levels of research and rigor is invested in creating these models, the good ones are typically built by looking at the highest performing employees and comparing them in some methodical way (data, collection, interviews, focus groups, etc.) to those of average or poor performance. After several iterations and a lot of input from business leaders and those closest to the metrics, a strong set of overarching capabilities and underlying behavioral indicators are forged. These behavioral indicators clearly distinguish the good performers from the poor performers and predict higher marks on all the important business metrics. On the other end of the spectrum, I've seen some companies just have a few HR people (who are relatively disconnected from the business) sit in a room and "knock out" a competency model. My point is, if you are going to use a competency model to identify some of your Level 3 behaviors, make sure there were some sound research methods behind it and some extensive buy-in from the business.

Competency models come in many shapes and sizes, and can apply to many different types of employee populations. You can have a broad-based competency model for all employees across an entire organization, or you can have a very specific functional model that describes a very small employee population doing a very specific job function every day. Obviously, the more specific the model, the more valuable it will be in helping you identify the right Level 3 behaviors. The larger and more diverse your population, the broader and more generic you have to be in describing your behaviors because they have to apply for everyone. On the other hand, if you have a very small group of employees working in a specific area of the business, you can be far more detailed and descriptive with your behaviors. For instance, competency models for large leadership populations may include behaviors like "Motivates others" or "Has development conversations with direct reports," while more function-specific models may include behaviors like "Conducts weekly ASI-3 coaching sessions with all customer-facing employees" or "Pro-actively uses PL customer database to resolve disputes." Whatever the case may be, the more directive and descriptive the behaviors, the more likely they are to be observable, measurable, and critical to the business. Also, the more customized these models are to a specific job, the more likely it is that the business has already bought into these behaviors and outwardly documented or deemed them highly predictive of success in a particular role. This buy-in will be paramount when describing your final story of impact.

One final benefit of tapping into a good competency model is the behaviors and descriptors are already highly visible and familiar to employees. That is, they are probably already discussed as part of formal performance appraisals and year-end reviews. This ultimately means they are vitally linked to employee recognition and reward. This makes a great connection in the minds of employees between the training content and performance, and increases the motivation to apply the learning and achieve the training objectives. As you'll see when we get into our Level 6, this perceived connection between training, doing a job better, and getting recognized for that better performance is one of the strongest forces behind the ultimate impact of your training initiative. Bottom line: if you find a proven, highly regarded competency model that includes observable behaviors that predicts business results, don't be afraid to take some verbatim bullets for your Level 3 survey.

Okay, so you've reviewed all the training materials, you've consulted with the business, looked at any competency models they have, and you've honed everything down to about six core behaviors that are measurable and absolutely critical to your business. Your raters will be able to observe *change* in these behaviors over the next few months and these changes will definitely improve some important business metric. Okay—all set with the behaviors? Great. Now you're ready to actually build your Level 3 survey.

Crafting Your Level 3 Survey

Your Level 3 survey should consist of two simple sections: one section for your *quantitative questions* asking raters to rate levels of improvement for the six–eight critical behaviors you've just created; and a second section for your open-ended *qualitative questions* to capture your success stories.

Quantitative Questions

Here, you will take those six–eight critical behaviors you've identified and simply ask about the improvement in each one. Whatever you do, don't be wordy with your question and just ask it directly like you were talking face to face with the survey-taker. Don't try to sound too smart and throw in a lot of words that only confuse or "obfuscate" (like that) the purpose of your question or the meaning of the responses. Also, remember to only ask about one very specific behavior at a time. This sounds simple, but probably 75 percent of all the Level 3 questions I've ever read or reviewed from all types of organizations are either way too long, include way too much psycho-babble, or are double and triple barreled. In these cases, by the time you finish reading the question, your head is already spinning and you want to dump the rest of the survey. For example, one executive simply wanted to know how competent his team leaders were at delivering difficult messages and negative feedback to their employees. The actual question that appeared on the survey wanted people to rate an employee's ability to:

- Summarize, synthesize and translate critical and potentially challenging organizational strategies and messages downward to employee constituents to ensure understanding and acceptance while creating an environment for open-dialogue?

What? Why not just ask about the leader's ability to:

- Communicate tough messages to employees?

My point is—just keep it simple and your survey-takers will thank you with more thoughtful and accurate responses.

Once you have all your behaviors/questions listed, just plug in your improvement scale for each one. Although there's some flexibility in the exact wording, your scale options should essentially range from *Exceptional Improvement to Got Worse*. Remember, it's important to keep a six-point scale here for the rater because the scoring on these questions will be the primary data you use to correlate your transfer

Table 3.1 Level 3 questions with improvement scale

Level 3—Behavior change

Describe your leader's improvement (if any) in the following behaviors over the last three months:

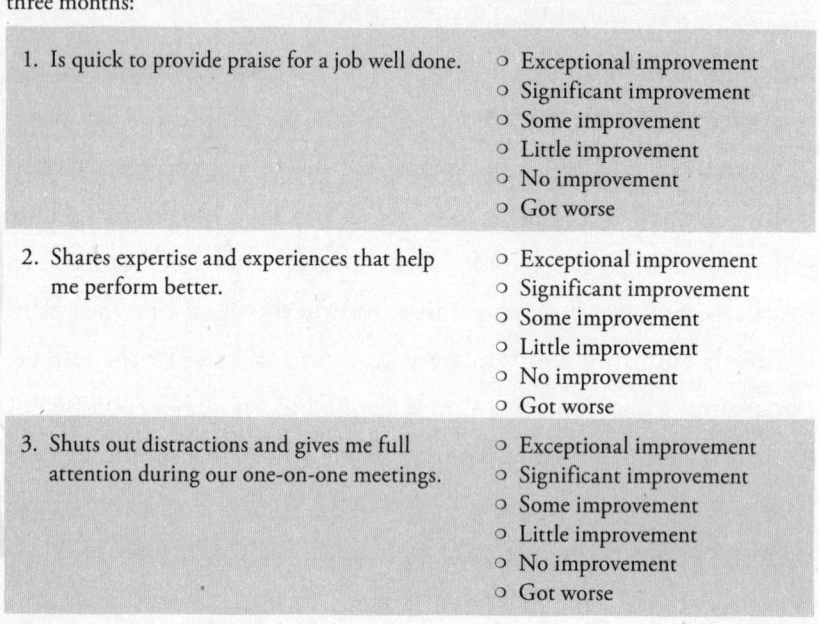

1. Is quick to provide praise for a job well done.	○ Exceptional improvement ○ Significant improvement ○ Some improvement ○ Little improvement ○ No improvement ○ Got worse
2. Shares expertise and experiences that help me perform better.	○ Exceptional improvement ○ Significant improvement ○ Some improvement ○ Little improvement ○ No improvement ○ Got worse
3. Shuts out distractions and gives me full attention during our one-on-one meetings.	○ Exceptional improvement ○ Significant improvement ○ Some improvement ○ Little improvement ○ No improvement ○ Got worse

climate questions and build your Level 6 analysis. That is, you'll take these Level 3 scores (a possible 1–6) and correlate them to your climate element scores (also a possible 1–6). Table 3.1 is an excerpt from a Level 3 survey I gave to employees to assess their leaders three months after the leaders returned from a two-day organization-wide leadership training program.

Reporting Your Results—Quantitative

When it comes to reporting the results of your Level 3 behavior questions, you're simply going to analyze and present the *response distribution* for each behavior with one or two headlines to sum up your data (see figure 3.5). These question-level distributions tell your audience how much improvement was realized by how many employees (reported in percent). It also breaks the responses

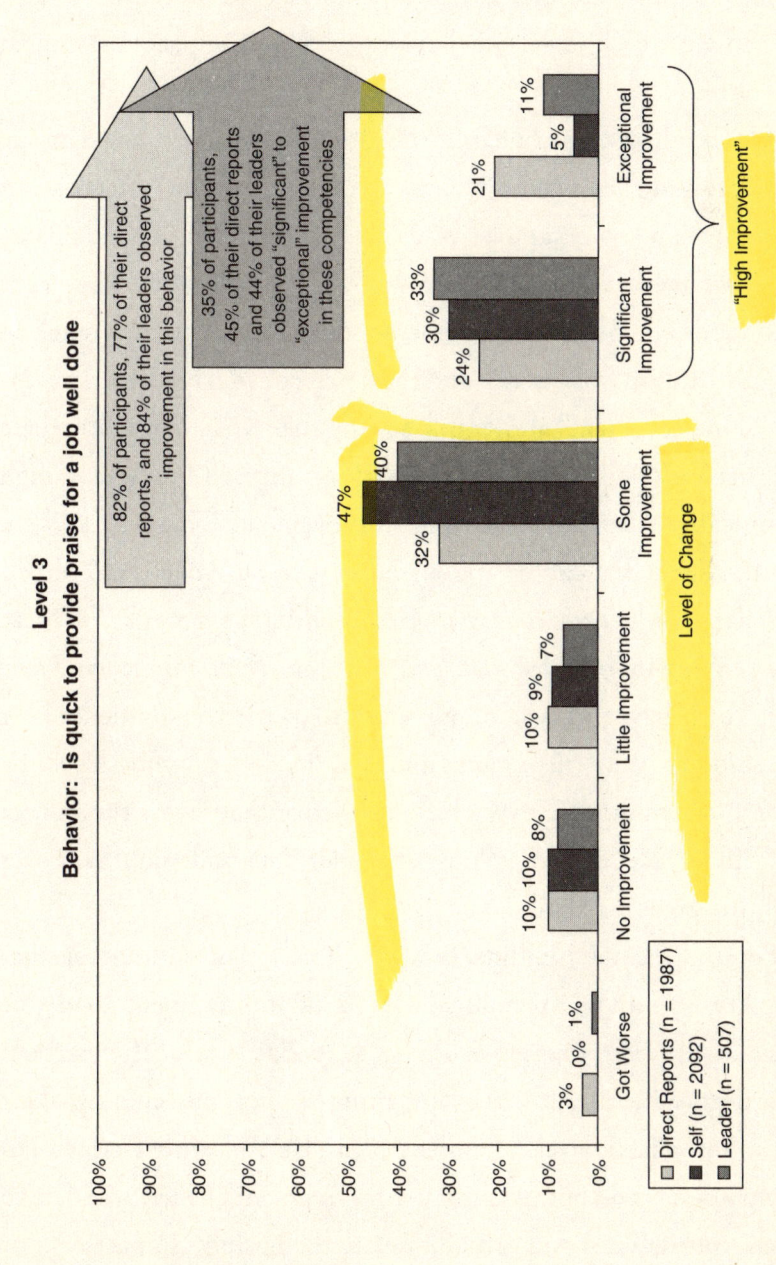

Figure 3.5 Response distribution for a Level 3 question.

up by different rater groups if you happen to be collecting leader, direct report, and/or peer ratings to corroborate participant self-ratings. These item analyses and headlines are particularly valuable to see which Level 3 behaviors are being impacted the most by training.

The headlines I included in the large arrows above the data are just summing up what I believe are the important categories of improvement. For example, when I say 82 percent of participants saw "*improvement*" (in the larger arrow), I'm taking the 47 percent who reported "Some Improvement," the 30 percent who reported "Significant Improvement," and the 5 percent who reported "Exceptional Improvement" and simply adding them together. Notice here I didn't include "Little Improvement" in my roll-up even though technically it can be considered improvement. This seems like a small nuance that can be argued either way, but believe me when I say that *being a little conservative in your estimates and calculations this early in your presentation will take your credibility a long, long way.* You'll have plenty of opportunity to dazzle your audience later on, so don't make them pause and question your numbers now by trying to scrounge up every bit of evidence that favors the impact of training. Never be frivolous with your data and you'll win over even the biggest skeptics.

For the second headline (smaller arrow), I'm adding together "Significant" and "Exceptional" levels of improvement to define what I call "*High Improvement*." Take special note of this particular category because it is the single most important building block for all subsequent levels of evaluation. In the following chapter, I'm going to show you how you can use this segment of employee data to create your Level 4 and actually isolate the business impact of your training. In the chapter after that we'll turn that business impact into money (Level 5). And finally, I will show you how to develop your Level 6 analysis from this very same set of data.

You'll also notice from figure 3.5 that the self, direct report, and leader ratings all tend to "hang together" for each level of improvement reported. This tells us that there was general agreement between raters and provides corroborative evidence that reported amounts of behavior change are actually happening. For example, few raters across all groups reported "No Improvement" while most reported "Some Improvement," and so on. I can't tell you how incredibly valuable this data is when someone questions the reliability of self-report responses. When they say, "Are self-ratings of these behaviors reliable and valid?" you can step up and say with confidence, "Well, you can see from the charts and data here that both leaders and direct report ratings are corroborating those self-reports." This should immediately squash any concerns your audience has about self-reports and their reliability.

After you've presented the results for each individual question, the next slide should be a snapshot summary of all the questions. This is simply an average (mean) of all the Level 3 behavior questions rolled into one. This aggregate slide will be telling your audience about average *overall* improvement for all the behaviors across all participants. This summary slide is absolutely crucial because it will be a key correlate to your Level 6 results. Figure 3.6 is a summary slide I used for an organization-wide leadership program. Notice I only included participant (self) and direct report data (employees that report to them) in this chart because for this particular training program, and the behaviors I chose, the direct reports were really the only group that were able to observe everyday improvement in their leaders (the trainees). Also notice that I listed all the measured behaviors right on the chart to easily reference them during my presentation.

Qualitative Questions

For the qualitative section of your Level 3 survey, you will ask for specific examples of behavior change and what that looks like in an employee's everyday work environment. Here, you'll capture all the

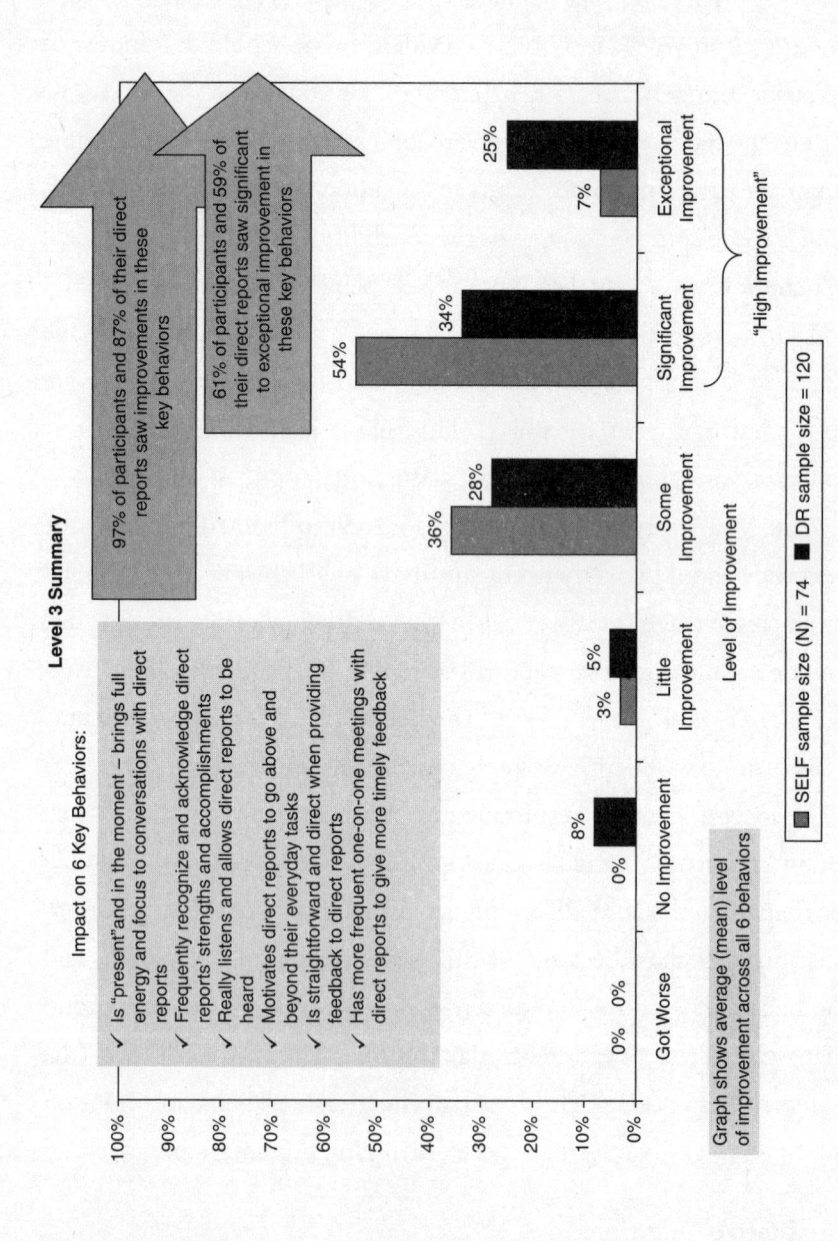

Figure 3.6 Aggregate slide for all Level 3 behaviors.

necessary free-form quotes and anecdotes you need by asking these *two simple questions*:

1. Which behavior improved the most?
2. What did that improvement look like on the job?

I know what you are thinking right now—How valuable and effective are these responses when it comes to presenting your results? The answer is simple—these responses and comments will be extremely valuable to your overall evaluation story *if* and *only if* you know how to use them. One of the biggest and most rampant problems with training evaluations is most organizations use these anecdotal success stories as their *only* evidence of impact. That is, they rely solely on this qualitative feedback to justify all their training investments. Unfortunately, these success stories without any type of quantitative data are just short of useless. This very prevalent reporting of just a few favorable quotes to justify a rather expensive training initiative is yet another reason why training evaluation has historically been seen as unscientific and of relatively little value to the business.

These quotes and verbatim inputs from the participants should *always and only* be used to add color commentary and a narrative to your quantitative story. For instance, when you are reporting and you say that 85 percent of participants improved a particular behavior, your audience will want some example or reference as to what this improvement might actually look like on the job. Give them a good example and they walk away thinking 85 percent is a great number. Similarly, if you first give them an anecdotal story of improvement, they will want to know what percentage of the population might have had a similar experience. Give them a high percentage and all of a sudden the story becomes memorable. The quantitative story will not at all be impressive without the qualitative, and the qualitative will certainly not impress without the quantitative. They should always be presented together and should be completely complementary of one another.

Reporting Your Results—Qualitative

To analyze and report the results of your open-ended Level 3 question(s), you'll use the same technique as you did for Level 1 and Level 2. Simply start reading though all the quotes, comments, and success stories. As you read through each of the free-form responses, start to categorize and bunch them into overarching themes. For instance, which ones talk about meeting more frequently with direct reports? Which ones talk about improving communication and influence with customers? And so on. This is actually called a *content analysis* and is more art than science. Here, you are taking specific examples/behaviors and bucketing them together into broader themes. Again, what you ultimately want to report are only the top three themes that come out of all the comments and then put some numbers to the whole thing by summing up the actual percentage (%) of employees who reported a behavior within each of your themes. Because you are only reporting the top three in your slide, these percentages do not always have to add up to 100 percent—many employees will give examples and make comments that have nothing to do with your big three. Similarly, depending on how much information your participants want to provide, you may end up with percentages that add up to more than 100 percent. This means that some respondents gave more than one example and described more than one on-the job behavior that changed as result of training. Either case is fine. My overarching advice on this whole content analysis is—don't kill yourself trying to fit every comment into a nice neat bucket. Your audience just wants a flavor for which behaviors are seeing the most improvements. An actual example from one of my reports, where direct reports are commenting on improvements they've seen in their leaders after his/her training, is shown in figure 3.7.

Level 3 Qualitative

What are leaders doing differently with their direct reports? (Direct Reports)

Top Three Themes

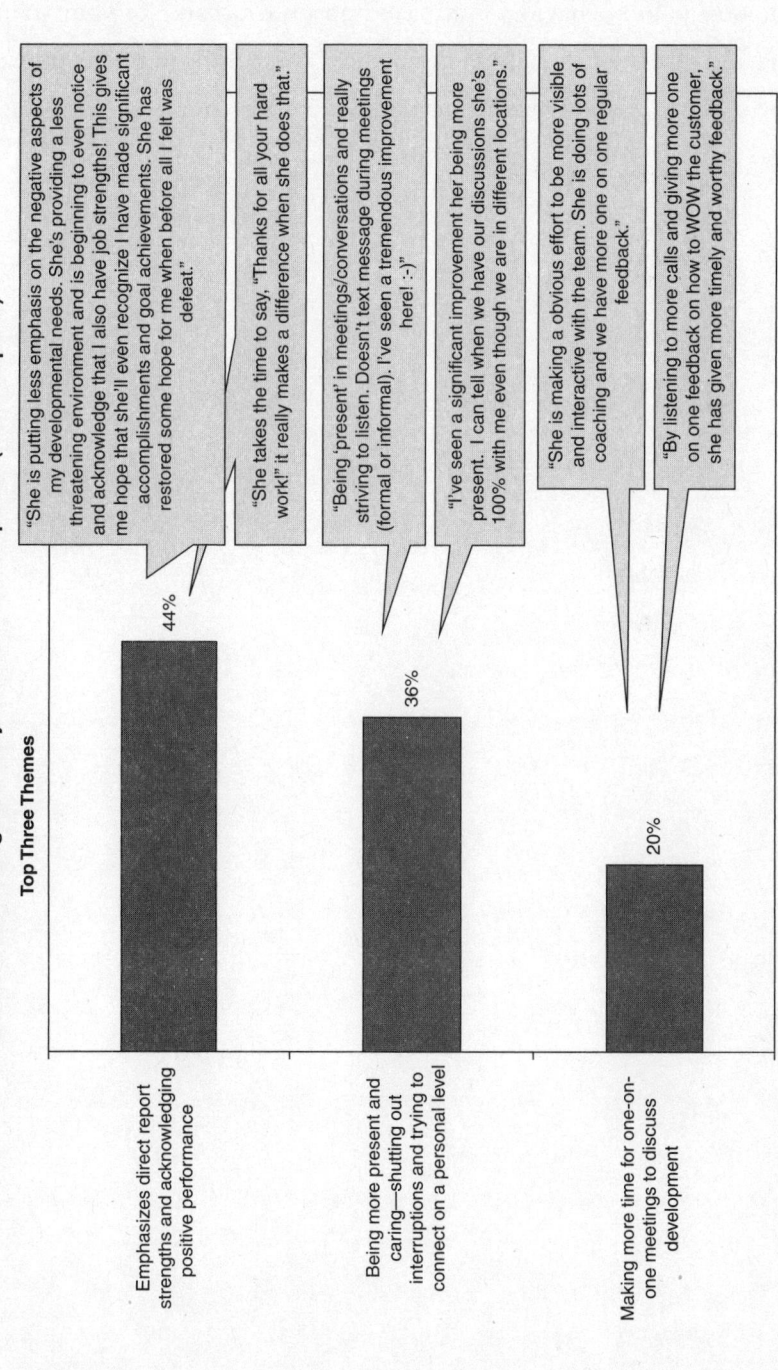

- Emphasizes direct report strengths and acknowledging positive performance — 44%
- Being more present and caring—shutting out interruptions and trying to connect on a personal level — 36%
- Making more time for one-on-one meetings to discuss development — 20%

"She is putting less emphasis on the negative aspects of my developmental needs. She's providing a less threatening environment and is beginning to even notice and acknowledge that I also have job strengths! This gives me hope that she'll even recognize I have made significant accomplishments and goal achievements. She has restored some hope for me when before all I felt was defeat."

"She takes the time to say, 'Thanks for all your hard work!' it really makes a difference when she does that."

"Being 'present' in meetings/conversations and really striving to listen. Doesn't text message during meetings (formal or informal). I've seen a tremendous improvement here! :-)"

"I've seen a significant improvement her being more present. I can tell when we have our discussions she's 100% with me even though we are in different locations."

"She is making an obvious effort to be more visible and interactive with the team. She is doing lots of coaching and we have more one on one regular feedback."

"By listening to more calls and giving more one on one feedback on how to WOW the customer, she has given more timely and worthy feedback."

Figure 3.7 Level 3 qualitative results from direct reports after a leadership training program.

Okay. We got through Level 3 behavior change. You've defined the on-the-job behaviors that have improved because of your training and you're now ready to define how these improvements impact the business. You've made it beyond the halfway point of your bridge and there's no turning back now!

CHAPTER 4

Did It Impact the Business?

How to Collect, Analyze, and Report Level 4

The inevitable question that will spring to everyone's minds after you show off your irrefutable evidence of Level 3 behavior change is...*so what*? How the @#$% does this impact the business? Who cares if Jane Employee or Joe Leader improves behavior X, Y, or Z?

This brings us to the elusive Level 4—Business Impact. What a Level 4 calculation does is translate your observable behavior change into employee productivity gains. How are the "new" or "improved" behaviors (the ones they learned in their recent training) actually impacting and improving an important business metric (some measure of employee productivity)?

Level 4 has a long history of being hard to measure and even more challenging to report. In fact, only about 5–8 percent of all organizations actually attempt to measure and create any type of Level 4 reports for their employee training. And quite frankly, most of the companies I've seen try it, don't do it very effectively. Probably the biggest roadblock and most frustrating question at this level is—How do I attribute any improvements in the business to my specific training program? That is, considering all the other things that can influence employee productivity, how do I *isolate* the effects of my training and define its real value to the business?

We all know how many factors can affect the health and performance of a business at any given point in time, so how can we ever confidently and legitimately say something like, "My training caused a 10 percent increase in productivity?" After all, any change in business performance could have easily been caused by a confluence of external factors like the market, customer preferences, business changes, and so on. And what about internal factors like reengineering, new performance incentives, or your biggest confounder—other training programs? That's right—if there is a bottom-line improvement in your organization, there will be a multitude of other training groups vying to take credit for that improvement. With all these factors to account for, it's no wonder nobody wants to report this stuff.

Despite all the challenges I just mentioned and the long history of organizations that don't report Level 4, the business of isolating and reporting the impact of your training is really quite simple. *All you need to do is demonstrate two things:*

1. When employees go through your training program, they improve behavior X.
2. When employees improve behavior X, it improves some business metric Y.

That's it. Sounds easy right? Well it can be. And if you notice, you're already halfway there. You've already demonstrated with your Level 3 results that your training has led to improvements in some important behaviors. Now all you need to do is link those behaviors to higher levels of "productivity" as defined by some important metric within your business. That is, are the employees with the most improved behaviors also seeing the highest improvements in productivity? And here's some more great news—You've already collected most of the data you need. Remember those categories of "High Improvement" and "No Improvement" from your Level 3 analysis? You'll be using those as your two comparison groups. Now all you need to do is compare their productivity, define the *effect* behavior has on productivity, and *Level 4 is done*. Taking this simple approach has led me to create some very powerful impact stories for some of the top companies in the world. So when it comes to calculating and reporting Level 4—fear not. In this chapter, I'm going to show you a brand new way, and in my opinion, the very *best* way to *isolate* the true business impact of your training.

Defining "Productivity"

So the first thing we need to do for our Level 4 is define what we mean by "productivity." What are the important business metrics or measures of performance and how will your trainees really be impacting them?

What Are the Business Metrics?

The first step you will want to take for your Level 4 is to find out which business metrics are most important to your participants. That is, how is an employee's "productivity" primarily measured? For sales employees it may be goods or services sold per month; for customer service employees, it may be customer satisfaction scores for the week; for assembly line manufacturers, it could be the amount of widgets produced per day; if you have a bunch of lawyers, it may be billable hours. You get the idea. Beyond these, if you dig even deeper, you may find another layer of metrics that is even more important to the business. For example, "sales revenue" may be broken out by product sales, service sales, membership sales, and so on—each of which may be weighted or valued differently by the business.

The next question you need to ask is—Are all your trainees from the same function and/or business group, with the same measures of success, or do they coming from diverse functions across the organization? If all your trainees are in the same business and are measured using the same performance metrics, your Level 4 analysis will be fairly simple and straightforward. If your population is mixed, bringing a wide range of performance metrics to your data, your analysis and reporting will be a bit more complex.

Either way, what's important here is you are able to define the productivity measures that matter most to your business leaders and stakeholders because they are your clients. Make sure your metrics are the ones they watch every day, every week, and every month. Make sure they can be translated into some quantifiable *revenue generated or cost avoidance* for the company. Remember, you will ultimately want to turn your Level 4 findings into Level 5 results. So always keep your eye on those metrics that will demonstrate a monetary "*benefit*" to the bottom line.

How Do Participants Impact These Business Metrics?

The next step in defining "productivity" is to determine *how* your trainees will be impacting the bottom line. There are essentially two ways this can happen: primary impact and secondary impact. *Primary impact* is where an employee goes through training and his/her behavior change directly impacts some business measure (e.g., a sales professional that increases sales performance). *Secondary impact* is where an employee goes through training and his/her behavioral improvements cause others (e.g., their direct reports) to impact some important business measures. The best example of this is *leadership training*. Making this distinction up front is critical to building the right methodology and measurement approach. In general, if your trainees are individual contributors that are close to the front lines, you will more likely be measuring primary impact. As you move up the organizational hierarchy and the focus of training shifts to influencing others, your measures will be more focused on secondary impact.

When it comes to the evaluation of impact, both scenarios have their strong points. When your trainees are directly improving a business metric like sales per month (by actually selling to customers themselves) obviously it will be easier and more straightforward to measure. When your trainees are leaders that are motivating others to increase sales per month, the impact might not be as direct, but can be far more powerful because the effect ripples out to multiple employees. For instance, in the first scenario, if a sales professional goes through sales training, the impact of that training is limited to that one individual. Sure it's relatively easy to measure, but it only changes one person's behavior and performance. It only increases sales per month for that one employee who attended the training (unless that employee is an informal leader or mentor). On the other hand, if a sales team leader or sales manager with ten direct reports goes through leadership training and becomes even slightly better at leading people, he/she can potentially cause ten employees to increase their sales per month. When leaders improve one or more aspect of their leadership, you can have a multitude of direct reports responding, being more engaged, and performing better on the job. So although leadership training and the analysis to follow can seem slightly less direct, the actual business impact and ROI can be a lot higher. In this chapter, I will walk you through both scenarios and arm you with exactly what you need to create powerful and concise reports for whatever type of training you're measuring.

Designing Your Level 4

Okay. Now that you can define productivity, you're ready to design your Level 4 analysis. Remember, the two things you need to demonstrate in order to say your training had an impact on the business are (1) the training improved some behavior and (2) that improved behavior leads to higher productivity. You've already proved the first part with your Level 3 analysis so now all you need to do is show the connection between behavior and productivity. In creating this Level 4 link or connection you will be doing two things:

1. Showing certain behaviors affect productivity. This is simply called demonstrating an "effect."
2. Defining just *how much* productivity is affected. This is called your "effect size."

In essence, you are first just proving the existence of an effect, and then showing how big that effect actually is. With these two results together, you will be able to isolate the impact of your training and define its ultimate "effect" on the business. Let's go ahead and start building this Level 4 link in our bridge shall we?

Was There an "Effect"?

To prove your training had a real effect on the business, let's start by looking at the only three employee comparison groups that can exist in your organization:

1. Employees who went through training and have reported significant behavior change
2. Employees who have gone through training and reported little or no behavior change
3. Employees who have not gone through training at all

When you look at these three groups, the first thing you might say to yourself is, "The only real way to tell whether my training affected the business, is to compare the performance of a group of people who attended the training to a group of people who didn't attend the training—right?" Wrong. The trained versus the non-trained "control group" is not the best way to isolate your impact. I can't tell you how many times I've heard evaluation discussions start moving in this direction and how I cringe when I think of how much time and data collection it may take for this ill-fated voyage. In my experience, the biggest and most common mistake I see made when attempting a Level 4 is using that third *Group C* (no training at all) in some haphazard, time consuming, and dreadfully doomed comparison analysis.

Why you ask? Well, it's because there are way too many confounding variables that can ruin the isolation of your effect variable. In other words, for this control group experiment to actually work, you would need to "control" for *all* the other possible internal and external variables that might affect the differences between these groups. Not only is this next to impossible, but you may need to send surveys to and collect data from employees who have never been through your training. Try getting the buy-in for that one from your business leaders. Again, the control group sounds good and scientific, and in fact might be a great method to study diabetic rats under monitored, laboratory settings, but it's an ineffective design for a dynamic organization with a confluence of environmental factors that quite literally change every day.

The best way to establish and demonstrate an effect due to training is to simply show that those trainees who significantly improved their behaviors are also the same ones that significantly improved their performance. That is, compare the first two groups (Group A and B from before), both of which have gone through your training.

Here, you will simply take the training group that had great Level 3 scores and the training group that had the lowest Level 3 scores and then compare how their respective measures of productivity changed after training. Think about how practical and easy this will be:

- You already have their Level 3 data
- You can easily add Level 4 data about their productivity
- You're already controlling for your confounding variables—the two groups will be similar in all demographics, business units, regions, and so on because they are all part of the same participant pool that took the training initiative

Are employees who are reporting great behavior change also showing significantly higher performance improvements? And conversely, are the employees who show no behavior change experiencing much lower performance gains? If this is the case, you just established and demonstrated an *effect* due to training. Got the idea? Okay. Now let me show you how to actually gather and analyze all your data.

Gathering Your Level 4 Data

You already have your Level 3 results from your trained population so now the question is—How do you collect their Level 4 productivity numbers? Here, it would be great if you had *all* the productivity and performance measures at your fingertips. You'd be able to correlate behavior change to productivity increases for every single one of your trainees and predict business impact. Wow—doesn't that sound good. Unfortunately, that's far easier said than done and having such easy access to the right performance data is almost never the case. In fact, trying to get all the necessary data directly from the business may prove to be a step that brings all your measurement momentum to a slow crawl or a screeching halt. It's been my experience, having gathered these types of performance metrics for over a decade, that the frustration of missing data, incomplete data, and the painstaking task of trying to match each individual's productivity metrics (captured by the business) with his/her Level 3 scores (captured by your survey) can absolutely decimate even the best laid plans and intentions. I can't stress enough how important it is to know exactly where and how you are going to get this data before you even begin your study. So the good news is I'm going to show you the quickest, most reliable, and practical way of collecting all the data you will ever need for your Level 4.

Want to hear more good news? We can get all the data we'll ever need by asking two or three simple questions. And want to hear even better news? We can add these simple questions to our Level 3 questions and get everything we need all at once. That's right. We can collect all our Level 3 and Level 4 data from the same short survey. No need to pull data together from different sources and pair up responses for each participant in your training. It'll all be right there in front of you in perfect columns and rows, on the same data sheet, on the same page. You can't get more practical and reliable than that.

Asking the Right Level 4 Questions

So what are these questions? When it comes to Level 4 productivity, you want to know two things: *what* and *how much*. Although the exact wording will be up to you, the first part or question (the *what*) should be asking employees about the primary metric or metrics used to assess their performance. The second part (the *how much*) should be asking about how much that metric improved over the months following training (usually three months). Here is where it pays to do your homework and connect with your business partners as much as possible before the survey. I say this for three reasons. One, you need to make sure you identify metrics or performance measures that participants can feasibly manipulate (increase or decrease) every day, week, or month with their discretionary effort. There's no use identifying metrics that don't change all that much over a few months or aren't directly influenced by the actions and efforts of the trained employees. Two, as I've stressed a few times already, you don't want to wait until your final presentation to get buy-in on all the right metrics to measure. If you don't understand their measures of success and which ones are weighted the most, you're sure to lose your audience. Three, if you do enough homework and you already know the *what* (the exact business metric) you can get right to the *how much*. That is, if you're sure your entire population is accountable to the same performance metric, you can simply include the metrics right into the question and ask your participants directly about their levels of improvement: *How much have your Global Sales increased over the past three months?*

If you haven't focused on one specific metric, but anticipate there will only be a few different metrics that can be impacted, you'll want to force your participants to pick the one or more that pertains to them. This would be the case if your training group is still relatively homogenous (e.g., almost all sales, business developers, or customer service professionals) and there's only a few possible outcome measures. Here, you might use a small drop-down menu and ask participants to first select their most important performance metrics from a few options and then ask them to report levels of improvement: *Which of the following is your primary measure of performance . . . ? How much has this metric improved for you over the last three months?* If you know your training population is very large and diverse, with a wide variety of performance measures (e.g., organization-wide people leader training), your first question will be more exploratory and then you will follow it up with your question about productivity improvement: *How is your performance primarily measured? Which business metric is most important to track your daily, weekly, or monthly performance?* and *How much has this metric improved for you over the last three months?*

Just remember, whether you do it with one question or two, make sure you've nailed down the *what* and the *how much* by this point and you'll have all the right data to do your Level 4 calculations.

As promised, I'm going to show you a new way to calculate your Level 4 and all you'll need are the answers to these questions and your Level 3 results. You don't even have to ask the participants for estimates of how much the training impacted their productivity. It will be a purely empirical comparison and the numbers will speak for themselves. In fact, as I will explain in detail later in this chapter, the biggest strength of my approach to Level 4 is that participants don't have to attribute any productivity gains back to the training at this point. As you will notice in the phrasing and implication of the questions, I simply ask, "How much has this metric improved for you over the last three months?" I didn't say "How much has this metric improved *due to training*?" or "How much has this metric improved *since training*?" I'm not looking for participant attributions here. I simply want to know how much performance went up. Then, I will let the numbers, correlations, and statistics tell the story of how they are related to the Level 3 employee behavior changes. If I keep talking about the training and how it profoundly altered their lives, I'm shifting the attribution and responsibility for all the improvement to the training event. And that just makes me sound like a cheerleader. A far more valuable story to business leaders is how certain employee behaviors lead to specific business results. Remember, the employee makes the improvement, not the training. And it's that behavioral improvement that leads most directly to the productivity improvement. As with Level 3, the connotation that you or your HR training team is trying to take credit for these improvements will only hurt your data. Believe me—no one wants to give any credit to the training event when they did all the work.

Bottom line—When you're presenting your entire evaluation story, the one thing you *don't* want to do is constantly emphasize the initial training at every step or level. Everyone knows that's where the journey began so you don't have to keep reminding them. And although the training might have been the starting point or catalyst, the real meat of this impact story is everything that happens along the way. You've already connected the behavior change back to the training, so now you just need to connect the behavior change to the business results—and that you can do without even mentioning the training again. It's crucial that you stay focused on these strong and contiguous linkages throughout your entire presentation. Remember, you're building a bridge, not magically transporting someone from one side to the other.

Anyway, let's finish these Level 4 questions. When you ask this question about productivity improvement, you'll provide your participants with a drop-down menu and simply ask them to *report the percentage of improvement* they've experienced.

How much has it improved for you over the past 3 months?
1%
2%
5%
10%
15%
Etc....

The options/increments here are up to you and what makes sense to the business.

Okay. So when you look at this question, the first thing that might pop into your head is—How can I rely on these self-reports and estimates of productivity increases for my Level 4 analysis? Well, the good news is your reliability is grounded in some very concrete and long-standing statistical principles. That's right—the infamous stats that we all fear are actually going to be our friend this time. Essentially, it comes down to three things: (1) sample size, (2) measurement error, and (3) homogeneity. I'll quickly explain all three here and then get into a lot more detail about the homogeneity of samples in the next section when we actually measure an "effect size."

In statistics, one measurement error, often called the *error of the estimate*, basically assumes that everyone who estimates anything will be inaccurate to a certain degree, but these deviations can be somewhat corrected for by other design factors. For instance, if you are looking for an "average" score, the *sample size* (number of people you ask to make estimates) is one factor that can greatly improve accuracy. Taking the *average* of *many* individual responses will be far more accurate than relying on a few to get it right. For example, if you were at a circus and everyone was guessing the weight of the bear in a sideshow, the first one, two, or even ten people might be way off with their guesses. But what if one hundred people guessed and you took the average of all one hundred guesses? What you will find is that average number will be extremely close (sometimes spot on) to the actual weight of the bear. In the same way, as your sample size grows, the *average* estimates of productivity gains will become far more accurate and your measurement error will begin to disappear.

The last factor, the *homogeneity* of your samples, will also do wonders to cut down your measurement error. This simply means if you are comparing two groups (i.e., our high improvement groups vs. low improvement group) you need to make sure that whatever can influence one group shows up equally for the other. For example, in this case, you may be concerned about a participant over- or underestimating their productivity improvement. However, if the two groups are equally susceptible to this estimator bias or error, you don't need to worry about it contaminating your comparison. In fact, as I will explain in the next section, this homogeneity of groups is finally going to let you truly isolate the impact of the training.

Analyzing and Presenting Your Level 4 Data

Once you've asked your quantitative questions and collected your responses, you are now ready to start your Level 4 analysis. What you'll be doing for this analysis is first looking at each participant's *Level 3 responses*. Based on these responses, you will simply separate your sample into two distinct categories—the "high improvement" participants and the "no improvement" participants. That is, you are taking all the participants who responded with "Significant" or "Exceptional" improvement on your survey and putting them in a *Group A* called *"High Improvement"* and taking all the participants who responded either "No improvement" or "Got worse" on your survey and putting them in a *Group B* called *"No Improvement."* Note, if your sample and responses are low for this Group B, you may need to drag in the "Little Improvement" category as well.

After you have separated the sample into these two critical groups, just compare how each group responded to your key Level 4 question (How much has this metric improved for you over the past three months?). What you will be doing here is looking for clear differences in the way each group answered this question. That is, what percentage of increase did each group see in their performance? How does Group A's overall productivity improvements compare to Group B's? Calculate an average (mean) of all the productivity responses for the "High Improvement" group and then calculate an average (mean) for the "No Improvement" group. Then compare the two.

Level 4
So what does "High Improvement" vs. "No Improvement" in key behaviors mean to the business?

[Bar chart showing "High Improvement" Group (N = 1174) at 38% and "No Improvement" Group (N = 244) at 17%. Legend: = Productivity Gains (average reported in %)]

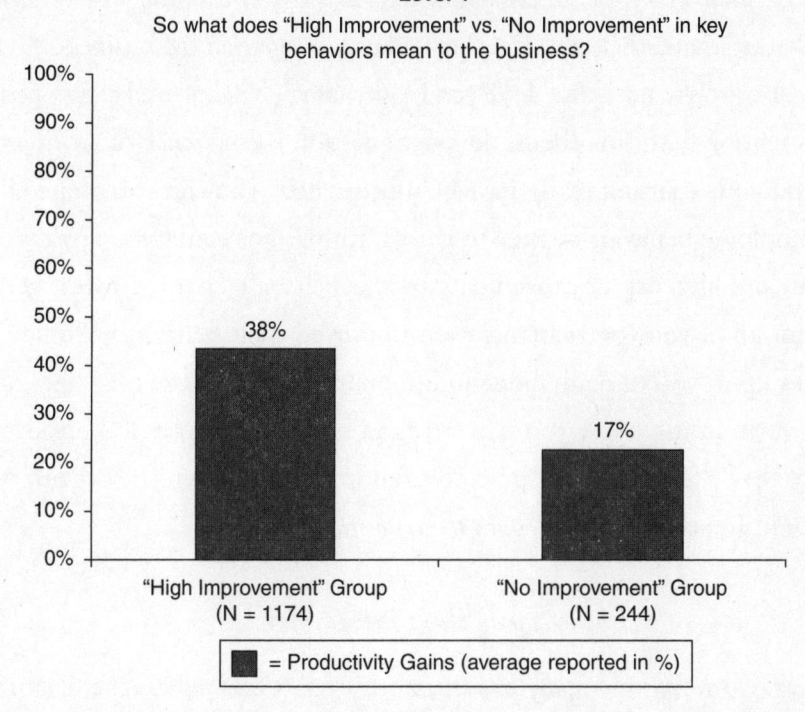

Figure 4.1 Level 4 analysis showing productivity differences between those who improved their behaviors (High Improvement) and those who did not (No Improvement).

Essentially, all you are doing here is showing that the participants who had significant improvement in their behaviors (Level 3 scores) are also reporting significantly higher increases in productivity (Level 4 scores). Conversely, the participants reporting no behavior change due to the training are reporting significantly lower improvements in their productivity. See figure 4.1 for an example of how you would present this compelling data for your Level 4 case.

As seen in the figure, on average, participants in the High Improvement group had productivity gains of 38 percent over the three months after training, while the participants in the "No Improvement" group had productivity gains of only 17 percent. This clear and significant difference shows that these behaviors actually "make a difference" and have a distinct *effect* on productivity. And since you already showed that these behaviors improved as a result of your training, you've just demonstrated that your training had a clear *effect* on the business.

But you're not quite done yet. Now that you've captured everyone's attention with this effect, the next question is *how much* of an effect did your training really have? Unfortunately, you can't attribute all employee behavior change to your training, nor could you attribute all productivity improvements to the behavior change. Moreover, not all of your participants even improved their behaviors. So now it's up to you to really hone in on, quantify, and *isolate* the effect of your training. Now you need to show the actual depth and breadth of that effect, and how much overall impact it had on the organization. In other words: *What's the true effect size?*

What Is the "Effect Size"?

Okay—we're now ready to isolate our impact and define the magnitude of the effect. In psychometrics or statistics, we might delve into something called a T-test for significant differences or an Analysis of Variance (ANOVA) to determine first, if there is a statistically significant difference between the two populations (Group A and B) and second, define how much of that difference is being caused by an independent variable (in this case, the Level 3 behaviors). While running these types of analyses are powerful and conclusive in laboratory settings, they often prove far more challenging and far less practical in organizational settings due to less controlled conditions and a slew of statistical assumptions that need to be met. So are you ready for some more great news? I'm going to save you all that time and analysis and show you how to define an "effect size" without all the elaborate and complicated statistics. With just as much power and accuracy, using the same two groups you just created for figure 4.1, you can actually isolate your effect size in three quick steps: The first step is just calculating the "effect" or numerical difference between your two participant groups. The second step is calculating the number of participants truly "effected"; and the third step is just multiplying these numbers to get your *effect size*: *effect X number effected = effect size.*

Allow me to explain. *For the first step*, to get your *effect*, just take the raw difference between Group A and Group B. So using the example from figure 4.1, the difference between the 38 percent productivity gains reported by the "High Improvement" group and the 17 percent productivity gains reported by the "Low Improvement" group is actually *21 percent* (38 – 17 = 21). This 21 percent is now the "*the average increase in employee productivity attributable to improving the key behaviors.*" Stated another way, "*If you apply the training your productivity can increase by 21 percent.*" And notice I say, "If you apply the training…" because both groups *attended* the training, but only Group A really improved key behaviors and applied it. See figure 4.2 showing the difference between groups.

Level 4
So what does "High Improvement" vs. "No Improvement" in key behaviors mean to the business?

"High Improvement" Group (N = 1174): 38%
"No Improvement" Group (N = 244): 17%
Difference: 21%

■ = Productivity Gains (average reported in %)

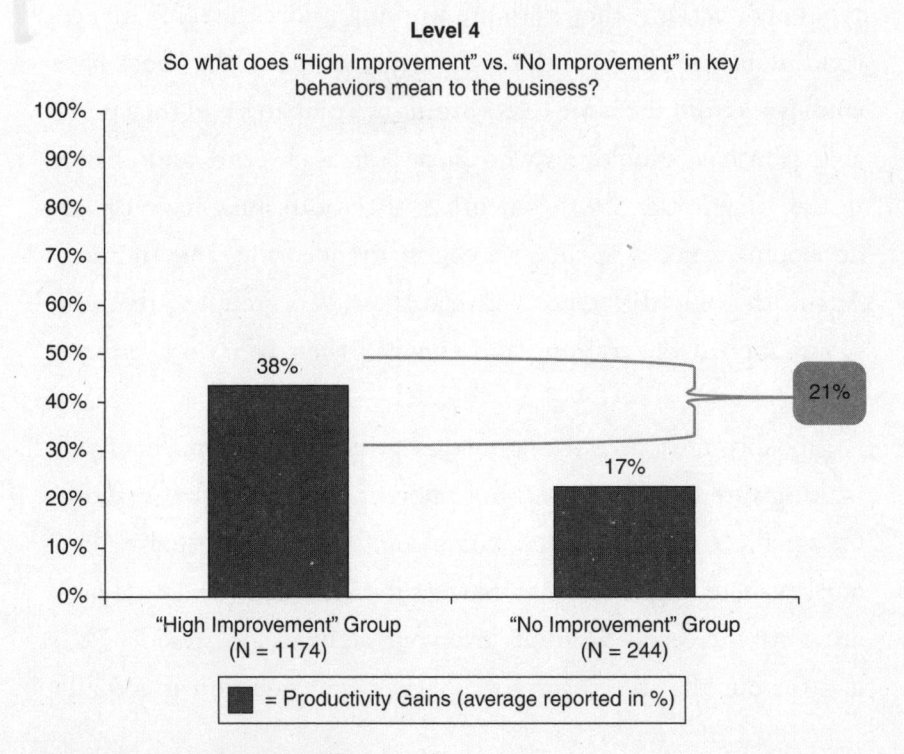

Figure 4.2 Calculating the *effect*.

The reason you can attribute this productivity difference to an increase in your trained behaviors is simple—your two groups are "homogenous." In psychometrics, one of the most important assumptions or criteria you need to meet when you compare average group scores is making sure they are similar on all demographics and variables except the one you are testing. As I mentioned earlier in the chapter, what makes this Level 4 design so powerful is the homogeneity or "sameness" of your two groups (separated into the High and No Improvement). That is, everything about these two groups is the same *except* that one applied the training and improved the key behaviors and the other did not. Under these conditions, your Group B actually becomes the perfect *control* group because it shares all the same environmental factors and influencers that could otherwise confound and confuse your results. They both have participants who are from the same types of functions, they both are working under the same market conditions, they both work for the same company, they both have employees from the same level within the company, and they probably even have employees who sit next to each other and answer to the same leader. Not to mention, they both must have similar development needs because they both attended the same training. Again, the only difference between these two groups is that one group applied the training and changed their behaviors and the other did not.

Probably most important to this principle of homogeneity is making sure that if any *bias* in responses does exist, that it shows up equally for both groups. For instance, as I suggested earlier, one bias here might be for employees to overstate their actual productivity increases. Wouldn't everyone want to look good? Well, it turns out that the "everyone" part of that question is actually the key to explaining away the bias. That is, because "everyone" may tend to overstate their improvements, this human bias shows up equally in group A and B. So even if both groups may tend to inflate their numbers what you can still rely on is the *difference* in averages between the two groups. For example, let's say Group A has a tendency to overstate their productivity metrics and the actual average is not 38 percent, but really 32 percent. Because everyone in the organization has this tendency to overstate their metrics, the average for Group B is not 17 percent, but actually 11 percent. Now, even though both of these averages were originally wrong, the difference between the two true numbers is still 21 percent. So, because both were susceptible to the same bias, the actual difference or effect is still quite accurate and reliable.

For the second step, to get the number of trainees "effected," you'll just go back to your data, count how many employees made it into your High Improvement group (number of participants who reported "significant" or "exceptional" improvement on their Level 3 questions), and then calculate what percentage they are of the entire population. That is, what percentage of participants from your entire sample actually applied the training and reported an "effect"? So as you can see in figure 4.3, as only 1,174 of the 2,468 total trainees in this example actually improved their behaviors, we can say that *48 percent* of the entire population was significantly affected by the training.

And for the third step, to complete your analysis, simply multiply the original effect by the number of employees affected, and *voila*—you've got your isolated *effect size. Level 4 done.* So using our example, we take the original effect (*21 percent* of an increase in productivity) and multiply it by the effected population (*48 percent* of trainees) and that gives you a total overall effect size of *10 percent* (see figure 4.4).

Level 4

So what does "High Improvement" vs. "No Improvement" in key behaviors mean to the business?

"High Improvement" Group (N = 1174): 38%
"No Improvement" Group (N = 244): 17%

■ = Productivity Gains (average reported in %)

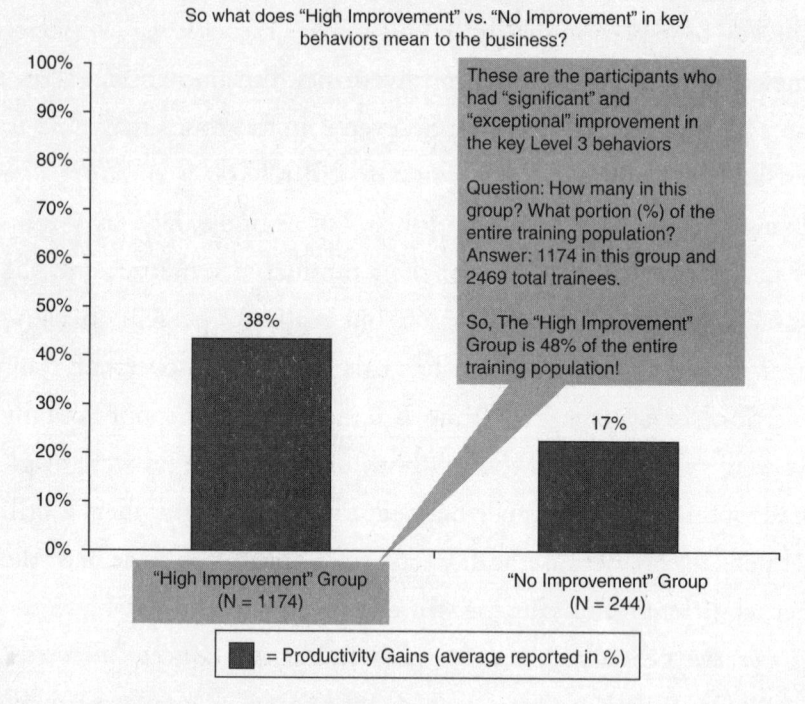

These are the participants who had "significant" and "exceptional" improvement in the key Level 3 behaviors

Question: How many in this group? What portion (%) of the entire training population?
Answer: 1174 in this group and 2469 total trainees.

So, The "High Improvement" Group is 48% of the entire training population!

Figure 4.3 Defining the "effected" population.

Level 4

% of employees effected: 48% × Effect: 21% = Effect size: 10%

"High Improvement" Group is what % of the entire population?

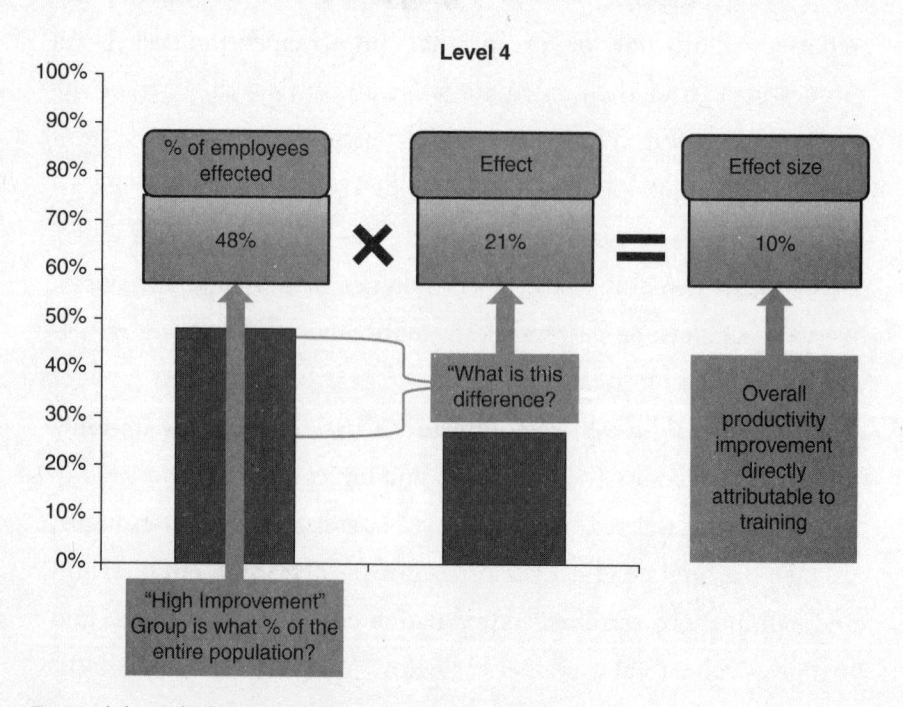

"What is this difference?"

Overall productivity improvement directly attributable to training

Figure 4.4 Calculating your effect size.

Thus, your Level 4 analysis tells you that your training increased employee productivity by an average (across all employees) of 10 percent. This 10 percent increase in employee performance is your business impact.

Ramping Up for Your Level 5

The question about how much this 10 percent is worth to the business is something you'll be taking into your Level 5 analysis to develop your ROI. Here in Level 4 you're defining the effect and impact of the training and in the next chapter on ROI, you'll be defining what that impact is actually *worth* to the business. Remember, you should be replacing the word "productivity" in figure 4.4 with the actual metric(s) your participants gave you in their responses. If your primary metric was sales, what does a 10 percent increase in sales mean to the business? If your primary metrics was customer satisfaction, what does a 10 percent increase in customer satisfaction mean to the business? But let's not get ahead of ourselves right now. Bask in the glory of your Level 4 for just a moment. You're now one of the elite few who know how to measure it right.

A New Level 4: Changing the Game

Calculating an "effect size" for Level 4 not only introduces a new method, but represents a profound and empowering shift in how we think about training impact. This new paradigm draws its power from doing three different but related things: (1) Highlighting the impact training can have when applied correctly; (2) acknowledging that some participants will be impacted by the training and some will not; and (3) shifting some of the responsibility and accountability for training impact to those who consume it. Let me explain.

Highlighting the impact of training when applied—Being in this game for a fairly long time, I can tell you that the number one complaint of HR professionals is that the business doesn't really understand and appreciate how much training can really impact the important business metrics. I can also tell you that the number one complaint of the business is that HR professionals don't understand how to impact those important business metrics. The simple reason for this huge disconnect is that everyone is focused on the training failures and not on the training successes. The harsh reality is that many employees go through training and end up having no significant behavior change and absolutely no improved business performance. The harsher reality is that everyone pays attention to and remembers these cases instead of the powerful success stories. By showing the powerful impact of training in the "High Improvement" group, you are essentially proving the value of training and demonstrating its bottom-line impact on the business. By linking Level 4 business results directly to training-related Level 3 behavior change, you are showing a clear chain of impact. This means the content and the overall training experience was indeed transferred to the job and was ultimately effective. This provides you with an important "safety net" if some businesses and/or participants claim or complain the training was not effective. You can simply point to this group that had significant results and change the conversation from "Was it valuable?" to "Why wasn't it valuable for you?" Demonstrating with hard data that the training does indeed "work" under the right conditions is the crucial first step in changing the perception of training.

Not everyone gets a return on investment—When it comes to training (and many other things in life for that matter), the only way to immediately diffuse the skeptics and naysayers is to acknowledge them and address their concerns. As I already mentioned, the ugly truth is that many employees attend training events and then return to their jobs none the wiser and no more effective than they were before the training. In these cases, their return on the training investment is actually negative. While the thought of wasting any money is troublesome, it is impossible to guarantee each employee a similarly successful transfer of learning. Whenever you send a normal population through any experience and assess them in any way, results will typically fall into a bell-shaped curve called a normal curve or normal distribution. This simply means the highest percentage of people will bunch around the average and the further you move or "deviate" from that middle average, the less people you will find. The people who are furthest on both sides of your curve are called the "outliers." These will be employees who had either exceptional impact and results from the training (on one side) and those who had morbidly miserable results from the training (on the other side). Acknowledging these "abnormal" employees and admitting there will be instances of wasted money and negative ROIs is the best way to silence training's critics and get the skeptics on your side. Once you've done that, everyone can start focusing on what really matters—the successes and how they got there. What was it about them, about their experience, and about their immediate environments that gave them such incredible business impact? And more importantly, how do we start duplicating those factors for future participants?

Shifting accountability for success—By showing business leaders and stakeholder that your training is effective under the right conditions and acknowledging that there will be a healthy mix of successes and failures in their group, you essentially pass the locus of control over to them. Now instead of asking for more training, less training, different training, or no training at all, businesses will be asking what they can do differently to capitalize on and maximize the impact of the training they do have. Now it's up to them to get the most out of their training investments. They'll be able to see how many of their participants are in the "high improvement" group increasing their productivity and business performance, and how many are in the "no improvement" group not seeing these productivity jumps. Being able to monitor and shift these numbers by focusing on their own training climates (which I'll show you in chapter 6) will become their priority. The raw amount or percentage of employees they can move from the no improvement or low improvement to the high improvement group will become a fantastic metric to track their success and increase their ROI. For instance, if the average employee in the no improvement group sees no ($0) benefit from the training and the average employee in the high improvement group sees a $10,000 increase in sales per month, the business can calculate the dollar value of moving one employee from the former group to the latter as $10,000. While they can't move employees who already went through training, this calculation applies to all future participants who go through the program. If last quarter they had 10 out of 50 participants seeing no improvement due to the training and this quarter they had only 5 out 50 participants seeing no improvement because they actually moved those same 5 into the high improvement group, they know they improved their climate and potentially added $50,000 in sales revenue.

Level 4 for Leadership Training

We just measured how a participant's behavior has a primary or direct impact on their productivity, but what about when the behaviors that they learn in training are meant to influence and improve *others'* productivity? That is, how do you create a Level 4 analysis for something like leadership training where all your Level 3 behaviors are improving leadership capabilities and not performance metrics? Here, the impact to the bottom line doesn't come directly from improving participants' own performance, but rather from improving the performance of their direct reports. The focus of this Level 4 will be the productivity levels of not the trainees (the leaders), but rather the direct reports that are being motivated and influenced by the everyday changes or improvements made by their leaders. As I mentioned at the beginning of this chapter, this "secondary" impact can often be far greater and end up yielding much higher returns. The crucial thing here is how you measure it.

As with our previous Level 4 analysis, the first step in proving business impact is showing a strong relationship between behavior improvements and productivity gains. That is, do leaders who make great improvements in their leadership competencies have direct reports who also make greater improvements in their performance and productivity? Conversely, do leaders who improve nothing back on the job (or nearly nothing) have direct reports who show reflectively lower levels of productivity gains? Again, to demonstrate this relationship, we use our handy critical incidence analysis. What this analysis does this time is separate the sample of *direct reports* into two distinct groups: Group A, direct reports of "high improvement" leaders, versus Group B, direct reports of "no improvement" leaders. Once separated, you again compare the productivity gains for each group and calculate your "effect size."

Calculating a Leadership "Effect Size"

To show you an actual Leadership Level 4 analysis, here's an example from one of my own evaluation studies: In this study, over 3,000 leaders from a financial company attended a two-day leadership training program. Three months after the training took place, I sent the direct reports of these leaders a short evaluation survey. On this survey, they were first asked to rate the level of

98 • Measuring and Maximizing Training Impact

Leadership level 4

[Bar chart showing Productivity Gains (average reported in %): Direct Reports of "High Improvement" Leaders = 42%; Direct Reports of "No Improvement" Leaders = 16%]

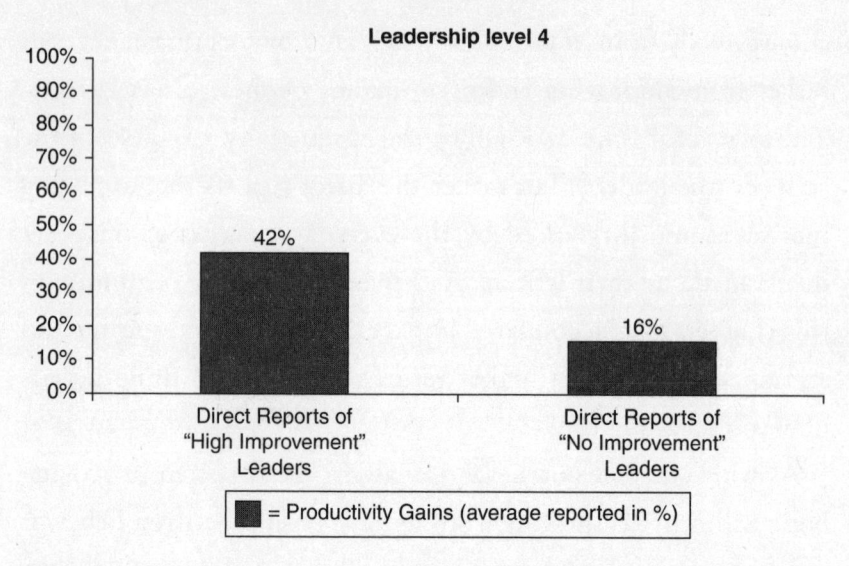

Figure 4.5 Level 4 showing differences in direct report productivity caused by improving leadership.

improvement their leaders showed in specific behaviors (Level 3 questions) and then asked to report the amount of improvement (if any) they saw in their own performance over the last three months (Level 4 questions).

When I received all the responses back from these direct reports, I cut the data into two "critical" groups—the direct reports of leaders who showed great behavioral improvement and the direct reports of those who showed no behavior change. I then looked at the extent to which each of these two groups of direct reports improved their primary measures of performance. Some very significant and impressive differences emerged. The direct reports of "high improvement" leaders increased productivity by an average of 42 percent, while the direct reports of "no improvement" leaders showed increases of only 16 percent (see figure 4.5).

Here, to determine the "effect" I simply calculated the productivity difference between the two groups: 42 percent − 16 percent = *26 percent*. I then multiplied that by the "effected" population (*45 percent*

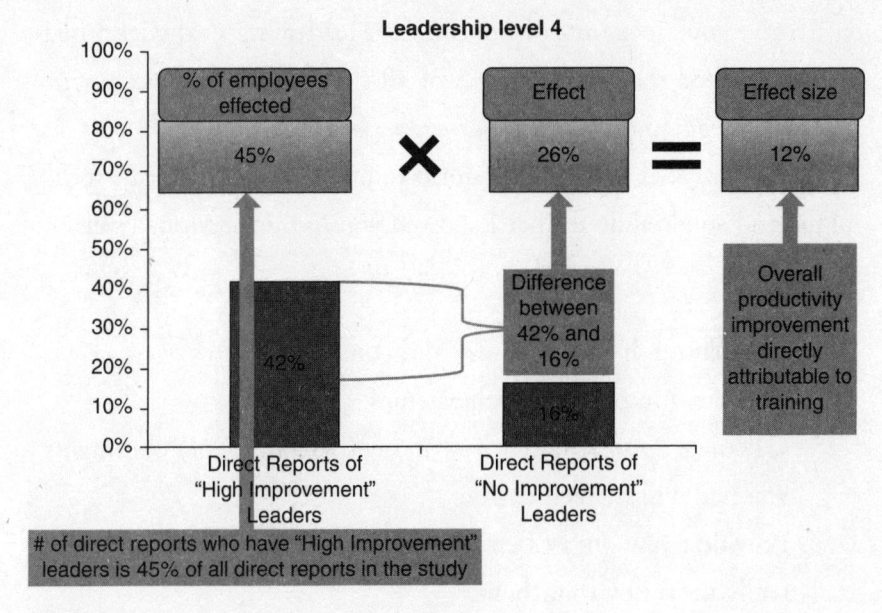

Figure 4.6 Level 4 analysis for a leadership program.

of all the direct reports had "high improvement leaders") and that gave me a total "effect size" of *12 percent (26 percent X 45 percent = 12 percent)* (see figure 4.6).

Level 4: The Qualitative Success Stories

Beyond your quantitative metrics and reporting, qualitative data should also be gathered to give a full and complete picture of your Level 4—Business Impact. As we discussed in previous chapters, the quantitative percentages and effect sizes without the *qualitative* "success stories" will be an incomplete picture of impact. The qualitative narratives and quotes add a voice to the numbers and make all the colorful charts and graphs far more powerful and meaningful to your audience. These success stories provide first-hand accounts of how new and/or improved behaviors directly influenced the discretionary effort and productivity of your employees. They essentially bring all the important linkages and numbers to life.

To give you an example from the same leadership study described earlier, I asked the direct reports of all the trainees: *Give a specific example of how you improved business performance.*

I then analyzed all these free-form responses using the same technique and single slide format I showed you in our previous levels of evaluation:

1. Read through all the quotes and comments
2. Sort them into overarching themes
3. Calculate approximately how many (percentage of) comments you had within each theme
4. Provide a few quintessential quotes to show what participants really meant by that theme

The main themes from all their responses, as well as some actual quotes about how their productivity was affected by their leaders are shown in figure 4.7.

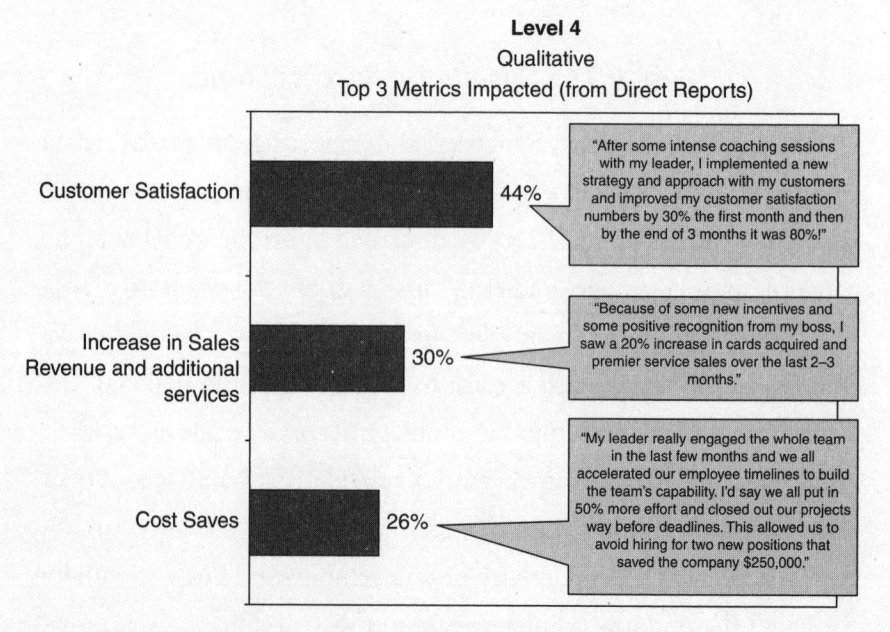

Level 4
Qualitative
Top 3 Metrics Impacted (from Direct Reports)

Customer Satisfaction — 44%
"After some intense coaching sessions with my leader, I implemented a new strategy and approach with my customers and improved my customer satisfaction numbers by 30% the first month and then by the end of 3 months it was 80%!"

Increase in Sales Revenue and additional services — 30%
"Because of some new incentives and some positive recognition from my boss, I saw a 20% increase in cards acquired and premier service sales over the last 2–3 months."

Cost Saves — 26%
"My leader really engaged the whole team in the last few months and we all accelerated our employee timelines to build the team's capability. I'd say we all put in 50% more effort and closed out our projects way before deadlines. This allowed us to avoid hiring for two new positions that saved the company $250,000."

Figure 4.7 Example of Level 4 qualitative analysis.

Ready for Level 5?

Okay. So you've got all your Level 4 results and you've built yet another crucial linkage or stepping stone in your bridge. You can now say, depending on what your primary metrics were:

- Employee Sales increased by 10 percent because of the training!
- We had a 15 percent increase in customer satisfaction due to the training!
- Training increased our speed to market by 20 percent!

Whatever measure of productivity matters the most, you can now state with confidence, and demonstrate with data, that you accurately isolated the effect and impact of your training on the business. Your next question, and the one that pushes us to the next level of our evaluation story is: *What is the benefit or monetary value of this increase in productivity?* Yep—we're ready for Level 5.

CHAPTER 5

Was It Worth It?

How to Collect, Analyze, and Report Level 5

This is it—ROI. Hopefully you didn't jump right to this chapter. Remember, Level 5 is part of an evolving evaluation story and should be extremely easy to present as long as you've already done a solid job showing there was actual behavior change (Level 3) and that behavior change had a measurable impact on some business metric (Level 4). In fact, your ROI is the part of your story that should have the greatest amount of buy-in because the important numbers and calculations that translate productivity improvements into monetary values should actually come right from the business. That is, once you've proven a certain metric increased by X percent, translating those increases into revenue or cost saves will be based on research and data that your business has already collected. While all productivity metrics might not be as simple and direct as sales, they all have their value to the business. Remember, if a business is tracking any metric closely, it's because they already know how much it means to the bottom line. For example, if they track the number of new customers they acquire every month, they already know how much money (on average) each of those new customers will spend. If a service business places a premium on customer satisfaction scores, they

Level 5 ROI Formula

$$\text{ROI\%} = \frac{\text{Benefit} - \text{Cost}}{\text{Cost}} \times 100$$

Figure 5.1 The ROI formula.

already know how those scores predict loyalty, profits, and growth. If a law firm tracks the amount of cases their lawyers settle out of court, you can be sure they know how much money they save with each case. With the right metrics and a solid case for Level 4—your Level 5 should be a breeze. Let's get started.

There's only two numbers you need for your ROI calculation:

- The *benefit*—the dollar value of your productivity improvements due to training
- The *cost*—the dollar expense of having participants attend the training

Once you calculate these two numbers, you simply plug them into your ROI formula and Level 5 is done (see figure 5.1).

Calculating Your Benefit

Let's assume you finish your Level 4 analysis and end up with a *10 percent improvement in "productivity" directly attributable to the training*. The question now is—How do you translate and transform this percentage increase into actual dollars for your company? This will be the financial *benefit* from your training.

Direct "Benefits"

Some metrics, like sales, are already tracked and reported in monetary terms so increases (or decreases) in employee productivity and performance are more easily translated into additional revenue for the company. For these types of metrics, all you need to do is take the *average* sales revenue for employees within your population and simply multiply that average contribution by your Level 4 result (percentage increase in productivity). This gives you the training "benefit." For example, one group I worked with had hundreds of sales professionals and after reviewing all their monthly performances, the average sales per employee, per month was approximately $50,000. I found from my Level 4 that the training experience increased their productivity (sales) by 10 percent so that meant an immediate "benefit" for the company of $5,000. Make sure you work closely with someone in the business that has access to and expertise in this employee performance data. You will need to know exactly what your metrics mean and how they impact the bottom line every month.

Indirect "Benefits"

Some metrics have a less obvious and less direct impact on the bottom line. To translate an increase in these metrics into hard dollar values will be a bit more challenging and require a little digging. The first thing you should do is connect with those employees who know these productivity metrics the best. Besides the business leaders and decision-makers, look for some of the front-line employees and those that are closest to these metrics every day. These may include internal analysts within the business or finance employees who just track and report these particular performance measures on a regular basis.

Start by finding out what type of research has already been done on your particular metric. Companies and internal business groups should already have a lot of data, previous studies, and even entire presentations to show that increasing (or decreasing) a particular metric is linked to greater revenue or significant cost saves. As I said already, if money comes in or goes out because of these metrics, there should be some solid research telling you just how much. If you think about it, the reason why they chose those metrics in the first place was because of some very compelling and convincing research that showed they are the most critical indicators of business health and performance. Believe me it's out there—you just need to get your hands on it. From these findings you should be able to start turning your Level 4 "productivity" percentage points into real dollars. Let me give you an example.

I was evaluating an organization-wide training program for a credit card company. The training population was over 2,000 customer service reps. The primary metric for these trainees was "customer satisfaction" or CUSTSAT and it was rigorously tracked on a monthly basis. At the end of my Level 4 analysis, I concluded that the training for these customer-facing employees increased customer satisfaction scores by 7 percent in the three months after the training event. So, the next question before me was—What does a 7 percent increase in customer satisfaction mean in terms of dollar benefit for the company? It sounded daunting at first, and both of the directors I was working with were skeptical about finding any internal research that directly translated customer satisfaction scores into dollars. But after just two phone calls, I honed in on a finance manager within the business who emailed me an entire power point presentation that described just how customer satisfaction is related to revenue. In fact, it was such a convincing and compelling study that it was presented to senior finance executives the previous year. It summarized two years of research on their customer satisfaction scores and gave me all the numbers I needed to calculate a dollar value for the training "benefit."

In essence, what I found in their study was the key correlation between customer satisfaction and increased "card spend." In other words, as customers were more satisfied with their interactions (with the reps) on the phone, they were also more likely to spend more money on their credit cards. In fact, from this correlation I calculated that a 7 percent increase in customer satisfaction would lead to a customer spending approximately $183 more *per year* on their card. Now, because I wanted to define that increase in card spend for only the *three months* after training (instead of a year), it actually came out to an increase in card spend of about *$46 per customer* ($183 divided by 4). This meant that if the average customer service employee could improve the customer experience and increase their scores by just 7 percent, they could essentially bring $46 more revenue per customer to the company.

I know what you are saying to yourself right now—"Hmm... $46 per customer—what's the big deal?" Well, how many customers do you think each customer service rep gets to interact with and influence every day? How about every month? Now multiply that number by the total number of customer service reps you put through training. Now are you getting the big deal? In fact, when I took the research presentation from Finance, factored in the 7 percent increase in satisfaction scores, added the number of employees that were trained, and then took the average number of customers impacted, the total benefit for the training was approximately $6,000 per trainee. With the total cost of the training at only $800 per employee, you can see why the executives were so delighted with their investment. Now that's an ROI. See figure 5.2 for a quick calculation of the "benefit."

Once you have identified your benefit (either at the individual or organizational level), all you have to do now is pit this benefit against the *cost* of your program, and you have your ROI.

Level 5

What is the $ BENEFIT of a 7% increase in Customer Satisfaction?

7% increase in Customer Satisfaction → Customer spends $183 more per year → Customer spends $46 more per 3 months × 130 customers contacted per employee = $5980 more revenue per employee per quarter → $ BENEFIT per trainee

- Training makes employee perform better
- Better employee = happier customer
- Happier customer = more money spent on card
- 1 employee can influence over 100 customers

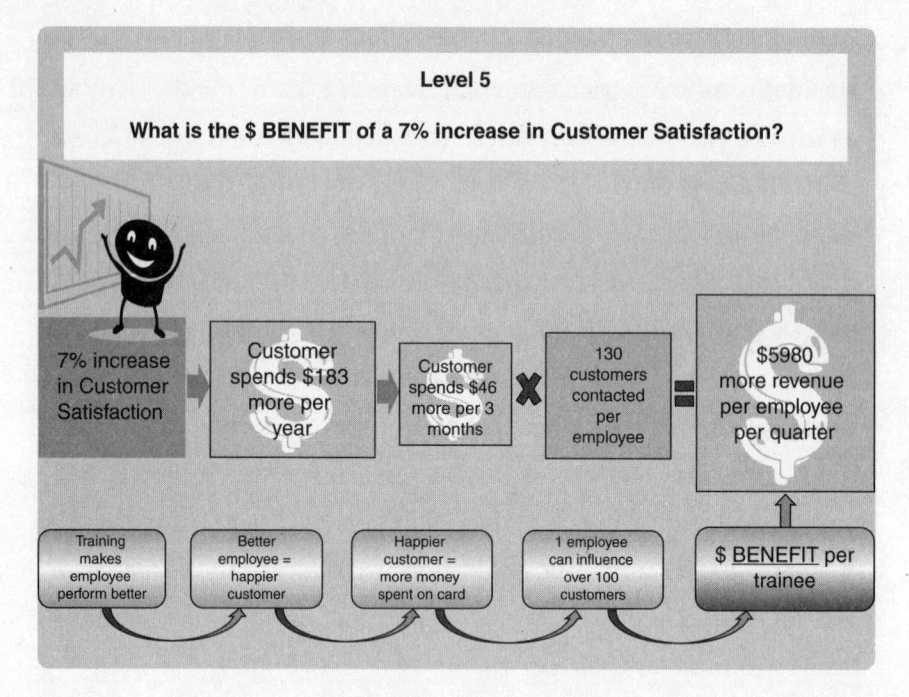

Figure 5.2 Calculating your "benefit."

Calculate Your "Costs"

Implementation Cost

The first thing you need to do is pull together all of the various costs for designing and rolling out your particular training program. These are your "implementation" costs. This should be especially easy if you have had a vendor actually charging and invoicing you for all their efforts to date. If you developed and rolled the program out internally, your primary costs would be the development of the program (including time spent by trainers and developers), creation of training materials, cost of booking conference rooms/hotels, and so on. You then just divide this total *implementation cost* by the number of participants. This gives you the total *implementation cost per participant*.

Invitation Cost

The next thing you need to do is calculate the average "invitation" cost per participant. This includes each employee's cost to register, travel, and physically attend the training event. Beyond the obvious expenses, be sure to include the cost of hours and days away from the office for each of your trainees. To do a quick calculation of trainees' costs due to "time away from job," just assume that an employee's salary per day = their contribution per day. Here, just approximate what your average trainee's salary is per year, then per day, and so on and then just add that total time away at training to your overall costs. For instance, if we assume that annual pay = annual contribution and the average trainee earns approximately $50,000 per year, then:

- 1 year away from office costs the company $50,000
- 1 day away from office costs company $150
- 1 hour away from the office costs the company $25

Okay. Now just add the *total implementation cost per participant* to the *total invitation cost per participant* and you have your "*total cost per participant*" (see figure 5.3).

Level 5

What is the COST of Training?

Implementation Costs | Invitation Costs

Development + Training materials + Rooms/Equipment + Misc.

Registration Fee + Travel + Time away from job + Misc.

Total Implementation Cost ÷ (Divided by) # of PARTICIPANTS =

Total Implementation Cost PER PARTICIPANT + Total Invitation Cost PER PARTICIPANT = TOTAL COST PER PARTICIPANT

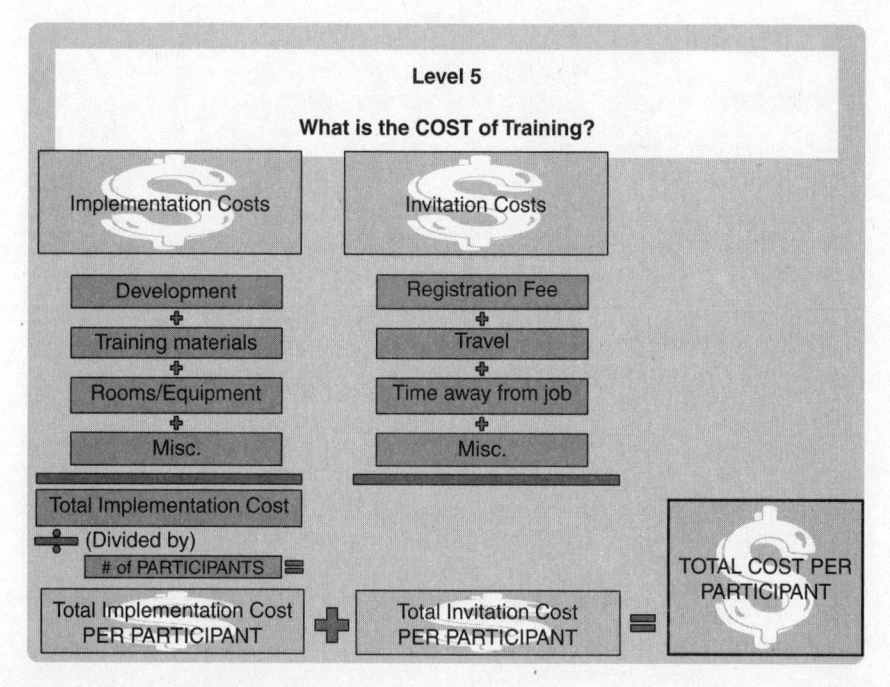

Figure 5.3 Calculating your "cost."

110 • Measuring and Maximizing Training Impact

Just to further illustrate this cost calculation let's plug in some real numbers using the same customer service organization that we used to calculate our benefit in figure 5.2. Here, when I added up all the development costs, training materials, rooms, equipment, and so on, the total implementation cost was approximately $250,000. To get that cost per participant, I just divided that $250,000 by the number of participants (2,000) to give me a *total implementation cost per participant of $125*.

The next thing I did was calculate the invitation cost per participant. This included a $400 registration fee for each trainee, an average travel cost of $100 per trainee (only some employees had to travel to the event), a few miscellaneous costs ($25), and because it was one day away from the job for every employee, I added an additional $150 per employee giving me a *total invitation cost per participant of $675*.

Level 5

What is the COST of Training?

Implementation Costs	Invitation Costs
Development $130,000	Registration Fee $400
✛	✛
Train materials $80,000	Travel $100
✛	✛
Trainers/Rooms $30,000	Time away from job $150
✛	✛
Misc. $10,000	Misc. $25

$250,000
(Divided by)
# of PARTIC. = 2000

Total Implementation Cost PER PARTICIPANT $125
➕
Total Invitation Cost PER PARTICIPANT $675
🟰
TOTAL COST PER PARTICIPANT $800

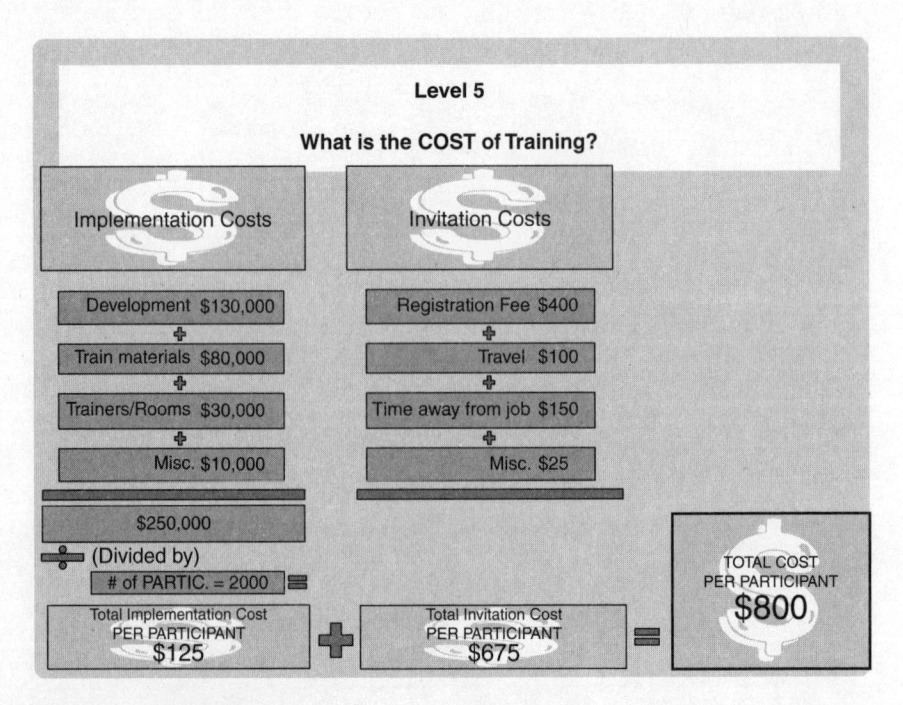

Figure 5.4 Calculating your cost.

Finally, I just added the total implementation cost per participant (*$125*) to the total invitation cost per participant (*$675*) and got a *total cost of training per participant of $800* (see figure 5.4).

Plug into Your ROI Equation

Before we plug our final benefit and cost into the actual ROI formula, I just need to take a moment, step up on my soapbox and scream and shout two extremely critical rules of thumb for your ROI story:

- Always "crunch your benefit"
- Never "cut your costs"

What I mean by these rules is if you are going to estimate any part of your benefit calculation, always err on the side of underestimating your actual benefit. Conversely, if you are going to estimate any of your costs, make sure you err on the side of overestimating and inflating your costs. You never want your audience to get the impression that you're trying to make your ROI bigger by either inflating your reported benefit and/or cutting down your reported costs. You'll lose them forever! I can't stress enough how just a little humble "investment" here, to gain your audience's confidence, will give you all the wonderful "returns" you desire. Always remember—with a conservative "benefit" and a slightly inflated "cost," you'll build great credibility and keep the audience on your side.

Okay. Let's go ahead and plug in our numbers. Using the same training example and calculations from figures 5.2 and 5.4, we plug our *benefit per trainee* of *$5,980* and our *cost per trainee of $800* into our Return on Investment equation (see figure 5.5) and *voila*.

Level 5
ROI

$$\text{ROI\%} = \frac{5980 - 800}{800} \times 100$$

$$\text{ROI} = 647\%$$

Figure 5.5 Return on investment.

ROI = 647%! What? Can our training really have a 647 percent ROI? Of course it can. And it should be that high. In fact, I would say that of all the large-scale ROI studies I've done over the years, the majority of them turned out to be over 200 percent ROI. The reason why these high numbers seem to puzzle, amaze, and/or raise a few eyebrows is because rarely or never before did these training organizations have such a thorough evaluation study to measure their true training effect. I would attribute most of this very prevalent dilemma to a lack of solid and accurate Level 4 results. That is, they had no valid and reliable way of truly isolating the business impact of their specific training. And without a good Level 4, they never had a chance at Level 5. The simple and unfortunate fact is they either weren't measuring at all or just weren't measuring things right. And when you don't measure right, you can't present results to your organization's leaders and stockholders. And if you can't present results to your leaders and stockholders, they'll never ever know how training really contributes to the bottom line. And that's what we need to change.

Another important thing to remember when reporting these ROI numbers is always remind your audience about the intangible and longer-term benefits that were not captured in your measurement approach. For instance, the "benefit" we assessed in our previous example was only for three month after the training, but these positive behavior changes and their impact on the business will absolutely continue long after the small time window included in our

ROI calculation. Even if you don't measure and include these types of longer-term benefits in your ROI calculation, don't be afraid to talk about their implications at the appropriate times during your presentation. This will remind your audience that you were actually being quite conservative with your measurement approach and your final ROI results. These are the breakout and sidebar discussions during your presentation that will bring even the highest ROI number into perspective.

Calculating the ROI for Leadership Training

When it comes to ROI, the training that can (and should) pack the biggest punch is your leadership training. As I mentioned in the previous chapter, when individual contributors increase their effort and show more positive behaviors on the job, they become more productive and their own performance improves. However, when leaders increase their effort and improve their leadership behaviors on the job, they not only become more productive, but they have a positive and tremendous ripple effect on all the employees they lead and influence every day. If captured and measured correctly, the "benefit" of these leader improvements can result in some stunning "returns." I call this the *"Leadership ROI."*

I can still remember the first time I presented my research on Leadership ROI. It was a room of C-levels, assorted business leaders, and other HR professionals. I could hear all their jaws drop as I described just how high their ROI turned out be. The study I described that morning was conducted over the course of one year and used a sample of 3,000+ leaders throughout the organization who attended one of the company's flagship leadership training programs. The objective of the training was to improve leaders' ability to diagnose the needs of their immediate direct reports, and consequently provide better direction and support as leaders.

For this particular study, it was shown that 85 percent of leaders were significantly and positively impacted by the training and were doing a few crucial things different after the training. I also found that these seemingly small changes by the leaders made their immediate direct reports far more engaged and productive on the job. In fact, these direct reports, on average, showed a 10 percent increase in productivity in the three months after their leader attended the training. I then pointed out that each leader who went through the training had an average of 12 immediate direct reports who were being influenced every day. That means that for every *one* leader that was attending training and doing a few things different, there were 12 employees that were enhancing their performance and improving their hard metrics by 10 percent.

Can you imagine how quickly and profoundly your ROI numbers can multiply with this type of ripple effect? Not to mention how this improvement and benefit could have cascaded further down to the next level of employees not included in our ROI calculation (the direct reports of the direct reports). Moreover, what about all the changes that lasted beyond our three month post-training measurement window? What about how this better leadership reduces absenteeism and turnover? Here's an example of how the "not to mentions" are actually mentioned but not included in your actual calculation. This reminds your audience how conservative your ROI really is. So while I didn't try to squeeze out a higher ROI by including direct reports of direct reports or estimating longer-term effects like turnover, I did include some of these intangible benefits in my talking points. This made everyone in the room feel confident and convinced that even a huge ROI number was still going to underestimate the true impact of the training. That's where you want them to be.

To make a long story short, I reported that this particular training initiative had over a 1,000 percent ROI. With numbers like that you better believe I went in there with some unshakeable data, some sound methods, and most importantly, a great story; a story that builds a *bridge*. As I walked my audience across this bridge, announced my ROI numbers, and gazed out upon the audience, I can see all the skeptical and confused looks slowly turn into smiles of acknowledgment and excitement. The results were clear and finally proved with real numbers what many of us always knew in our guts already—some leadership training really works. Now there was no denying the incredible power that a few small changes by a few powerful leaders can have on the bottom line. This is the power of the Leadership ROI.

Ready for Level 6?

We did it. We've thoroughly covered evaluation Levels 1–5 and now you know how to build a strong and direct path from the training event all the way to ROI. But our bridge isn't quite done yet. Measuring the traditional Levels 1–5 is a spectacular accomplishment, but these levels only tell part of the story. My next question is—How do we use our new measurement expertise to actually *improve* the impact of training? Now that we know how to measure whether training "works" or not, maybe we can finally find out why it works better for some and worse for others. Maybe by uncovering these factors, we can increase the effectiveness of training in the future. After all, the final results you get from training are really a function of two things—the *training* itself *and* the *climate* in which you apply the training.

Imagine if you were training for years to be an incredible pitcher and then on your major league opening day it was raining. How about if your coach sat you on the bench? It doesn't matter how good you are or how hard you trained—*the "climate" wouldn't let you pitch!* In all the same ways, we are constantly sending employees through training and then letting them go into an environment where something is preventing them from changing, improving, and truly maximizing their return on investment. Now that we have a solid and sensitive measurement approach, we are in the perfect position to explore and measure these *climate* factors to really understand the things in our employees' immediate work environment that are either helping or hindering the true impact of training.

This brings us, in my opinion, to the most critical and most powerful of all evaluation levels—Level 6—Transfer Climate. Let's face it, measuring the effects and bottom-line impact of training is exciting for any business leader, but being able to identify the hardwiring of what really makes your training work back on the job can be a complete game-changer for your entire organization. Get ready to identify and measure the things in your employees' work day that can truly make or break all of your training efforts. Get ready to measure your Level 6.

CHAPTER 6

How Do We Maximize Impact?

How to Collect, Analyze, and Report Level 6

Level 6—What Is It?

Level 6 is an evaluation that simply measures your climate and tells you which environmental factors are most affecting the impact of your training. In my introduction, I referred to these important factors as the critical *pillars* of your bridge. I called them critical because without these strong and sturdy support structures, everything you built up to now, including all the solid linkages you created with your Levels 1–5, will crumble and disappear right under your feet. In order to build these pillars right and make your bridge strong enough to support your travelers (trainees), you must understand and anticipate the *climate* factors that can shake your bridge and threaten their journey. That is, what are the environmental factors (things that are happening in the employee's immediate work environment) that are either supporting or sabotaging the impact of training back on the job? Once you know which climate factors are causing your training to succeed or fail, you as the architect can then design and construct a stronger, more effective bridge. This fortified bridge will then keep employees safe as they traverse the treacherous path from training to business results, and help them avoid the many pitfalls that all too often cause training to fail.

I call this Level 6 a "Transfer Climate" analysis because it tells us exactly which *climate* factors are most important when employees attempt to *transfer* what they learned in training back to their everyday jobs. In fact, the amount of behavior change, productivity improvement, and return on investment that all participants are able to achieve will solely and absolutely depend on the success of this transfer. And after many years of research with over 20,000 participants, I can say with absolute confidence that these climate elements are so powerful at predicting the overall impact of your training that they can quite literally "make or break" your entire initiative.

Okay. What are some examples of these make or break climate factors? What are the types of things in your employees' (trainees') immediate work environment that are fostering or frustrating the effects and overall impact of your training? While climate factors can be as diverse as the organizations that host them, there are essentially only two main types of factors that are always creating and contributing to every employee's climate:

1. *People factors*—other employees (e.g., leader and coworkers) that influence the trainee every day
2. *Organizational factors*—normal structures in the organization (e.g., job roles, hierarchies, and policies) that influence the trainee every day

Let me give you an example of each: If you just took the most thought-provoking and inspirational training on innovation, but then returned to your job and your immediate leader told you to keep doing things the way you always have, your leader's lack of support is a climate factor (a *people factor*) that is crippling your successful transfer and preventing your training from having any measurable business impact. If you just spent three days and a $1,000 in T&E at an off-site training event to make you a better sales professional, but then returned to an environment or compensation system that did not pay for performance and incentivize greater sales, this lack of a formal reward system is a climate factor (an *organizational factor*) that is hindering your transfer and stifling your potential business impact.

Just citing the examples mentioned earlier, I'm sure you must be thinking to yourself right now, "How can we ever identify and account for all the possible climate elements that may be influencing our trainees when they return to their own unique work environments?" After all, for each employee these climate factors may or may not exist, exert varying degrees of influence, and even combine and interact in unpredictable ways. Where do we start and how do we make sense of these transfer climates in our organizations?

The answer is simple. You need to forget about identifying *every* climate factor that can be influencing your employees' training and just identify the most *critical* factors. Which factors are helping or hindering your training transfer the most? Which are the most powerful at predicting your trainees' behavior change, business impact, and ROI? This is where your Level 6 evaluation comes in And the good news is you don't have to start from scratch. By sharing some of my own research, by showing you how to do your own analysis, and by giving you some examples of how to present your results, you will be fully ready to evaluate and report on the optimal transfer climates within your own organization. And some more good news is that these climate elements tend to be fairly conspicuous, pervasive, and consistent in their influence across all training programs within a given organization. That is, once you identify your most important people and organizational climate factors, they can then be used to boost and maximize the impact of any training program. That's right—*once you evaluate and adjust the climate, you will then get more bang for your buck for all your training initiatives.*

After many years of presenting impact studies, I have yet to encounter a business group or client that does not find this Level 6 evaluation the most interesting and informative piece of the overall results presentation. Measuring Levels 1–5 is critical, but if you stop there it makes you look more like a cheerleader trying to prove the value of your training rather than an objective researcher and consultant who can help an organization understand the factors that make or break the impact and sustainability of their training over time. In fact, from a client perspective, they may already assume you have an agenda or vested interest in the positive outcomes of a training program. They may be expecting you to sing its praises as you present all your evaluation results. In this case, great results are not surprising and no matter how long you stand there touting all the benefits, you'll eventually lose your audience. To keep them at the edge of their seats, you've got to tell them *why* their training works and give them results that they can use to *evolve* their training strategies for the future.

What can they learn from your training evaluation and how can they use your research findings to continually improve their initiatives and roll out solutions that are more effective in the future? Can you provide them with the critical follow-up they need to help them evolve and learn as a *business*? Can you tell them why the training worked better for some employees as opposed to others? Why did some training dollars see returns of 500 percent while others were a horrible waste? Imagine presenting your research and being able to answer all these questions If you think about all the immediate benefits from a client's perspective, you'll understand why your audience will become genuinely excited about this additional level of evaluation.

So before I jump into exactly how to do your Level 6 analysis, let me just share a short summary of these benefits as experienced and expressed by my own audiences as I presented these analyses over the years.

Benefits of Level 6

Level 6 Is Future-Oriented

As I stated before, measuring the traditional five levels of evaluation (1—Participant Reaction to 5—ROI) is a rare and amazing accomplishment, but unfortunately, these five levels don't tell the most dynamic part of the story. That is, they tell you if training "worked" or "didn't work" in the past tense, but don't tell you how to improve impact and make the same training more successful in the future. Adding a Level 6 makes training evaluation dynamic and forward-looking because it tells you how to change your results over time. It instantly turns evaluation from an afterthought into an evolving story that applies and plugs all your data into a strategy of continuous improvement. It ultimately tells your clients and shareholders—this is the climate you need to create to really drive impact and maximize your training dollars in the future.

Level 6 Is Action-Oriented

Once you identify the right climate and environment for transfer back on the job, there is an immediate *call to action*. In order for training to be as effective as it can be, something must now be done to improve the climate. And the best part about this call to action is a large amount of the action and accountability for fostering that climate falls squarely on the shoulders of the business leaders and clients. It puts the power to change and improve training results back in the hands of the clients and business leaders because now they understand what role they play and how they can maximize their own training results. In fact, one of the biggest ah-ha moments I had as I started putting my results in front of business leaders was—there's only one thing they like more than hearing about results and that's telling them how they can improve those results.

By focusing on and assessing what happens when employees return to their jobs, desks, cubicles, and coworkers, you are inherently (and justifiably) shifting a lot of the accountability for "successful" training to the business leaders. They are ultimately the ones that can create and drive the right "transfer climates" back on the job. They are the ones that can create the right environments for employees to practice, apply, and sustain what they have learned in training. After all, the business leaders spend a lot of money putting their employees through training—isn't it only fair that we give them some control over the outcome?

Level 6 Explains the Variability of Results

"Hey! What happened? We spent a lot of money and the training didn't work for us!" Whoever and wherever you are in the training industry, you've probably spent a sleepless night or two worried about hearing this one. Well fear no more! With the right Level 6 analysis in place, you will be able to explain the variability of results within and across your training population. There's always going to be individuals for whom the training does not work and there's always going to be those individuals who had a great experience and cranked up their performance. The Level 6 climate evaluation arms you as the training professional with a crucial piece of information—why training works for Mary and not for Joe? Why did it really work wonders for some teams and fall flat for others? By analyzing and identifying disparate climates within your training population, and showing how they affect training outcomes, you are able to explain why some participants succeed while others fail. Next time a business leader comes to you or your training group and says, "Why didn't the training work?" you can confidently respond, "Well it worked for this other group—they had a great ROI. Let's examine your climate and see how it compares to this other group. And most importantly, let's see what we can do to fix it."

Level 6 Increases ROI!

It makes you more money! Hello! If you know which climate elements will maximize your ROI, you can begin providing the support and tools to make a positive climate shift. You now know where to focus your change efforts and can get to the very serious business of shaping the post-training environment in ways that will get you the greatest return on your training dollars. In fact, by boosting just a few key factors, you can create a climate that will improve the impact and ROI of virtually any training program. This means continued performance gains and higher returns on all your future training. Which are the strongest predictors of success and how much is improving each one ultimately going to be worth to the organization? A solid Level 6 will tell you the weight of each of your factors and help you prioritize the ones that will make the biggest splash and ultimately get you the highest returns.

Alright, I will assume you're convinced of the benefits by this point so I'll jump right into *how* you can build and measure your Level 6.

Collecting Your Level 6 Data

Create a Transfer Climate Assessment

The first thing you'll need to do to identify your most critical climate factors is to develop what I call a Transfer Climate Assessment. This is simply a list of possible suspects that you believe are either helping or hindering participants from transferring their learning back to the job. Fortunately, you don't have to start from scratch. After drawing from decades of research on the topic of "learning transfer" and conducting over ten years of training impact and transfer studies myself, I believe I've managed to hone in on what I consider the most powerful and most "usual suspects."

The assessment I created consists of 12 climate items that I've found to be the most predictive of training impact across all training programs, organizations, and levels of employees. Whether it was a leadership program for executives, a sales program for service reps, or technical training for finance managers, these climate factors were the strongest influencers of resultant business impact and ROI. While many others were included (and significant) in my earlier evaluation studies, the list of factors I've created here turned out to be the most significant and conspicuous "make or break" factors in the bunch. See table 6.1 and a description of each factor.

Table 6.1 Twelve factors for your climate assessment

1. I meet with my leader one-on-one to discuss how I can apply my training on the job
2. I expect my leader to recognize and reward me for applying the training and making improvements
3. My leader expresses his/her support and endorsement for the training
4. I can "try out" new behaviors or practices on the job without fear of sanctions or negative consequences
5. My coworkers encourage me to "go above and beyond" current levels of performance
6. I have the time and opportunity to apply these training behaviors on the job
7. It's clear to me how applying this training will increase the metrics that really matter to my business
8. My leader advocates for my development and wants me to advance in this company
9. I really want to apply the behaviors I learned in training.
10. The behaviors taught in the training are extremely relevant to my specific job role
11. I will get compensated for my productivity improvements
12. I am committed to the success of this company

1. *I meet with my leader one-on-one to discuss how I can apply my training on the job.* When participants meet with their immediate managers to discuss the training, they make critical connections between the content of the training and what's expected of them in their roles. These one-on-one conversations help define what behaviors should change as results of the training and, more importantly, which business metrics those behaviors are expected to impact. Ideally, the participant and leader should meet at least once before the training event to discuss the expected outcomes on the job and then plan to meet regularly after the training (e.g., once a week) to check for progress and improvement in these behaviors and metrics. The initial meeting gives the participant and the leader the opportunity to take the more generic behaviors listed in the training objectives and hone them down to very specific behaviors/objectives relevant to a participant's everyday roles and responsibilities. What will change and improve over the next few months following training and what will that improvement look like for John? What will that look like for Jane? Participant and leader should agree on at least three very specific, business critical behaviors and then "contract" for improvement. The best part about identifying and detailing these specific behaviors is it gets participants and leaders on the same page as far as what constitutes "improvement" over the next few months. The one-on-one meetings should continue over the next 12 weeks with manager and trainee devoting at least 15 minutes or so during their already scheduled updates to just talk about the training impact.
2. *I expect my leader to recognize and reward me for applying the training and making improvements.* Recognition and reward are the key to motivating on-the-job change and improvement.

And almost always, the immediate manager or leader has the first opportunity to dish it out. Once the employee starts to improve his/her behaviors and the objectives of the training are being achieved, the leader needs to be frequent and consistent in acknowledging the improvements and providing incentives. Even though most leaders are constrained in their ability to dole out frequent formal rewards (e.g., monetary performance-based incentives, monthly commissions, etc.), there's nothing preventing them from being liberal and generous with the informal rewards (e.g., praise, recognition during team meetings, organizational announcements of outstanding improvement, etc.). The key here is that all these rewards are tightly linked to and contingent on the improvements that happened because the training was applied. One way to ensure these training-related behaviors are rewarded would be to align them with the behaviors or competencies that are already formally recognized and rated in annual performance appraisals. Any time this alignment is possible, and participants can see the clear connection between training and formal performance appraisals, the training will likely have greater impact.

3. *My leader expresses his/her support and endorsement for the training.* Getting a solid sense that your leader believes in the training and sees the business benefits of you taking valuable time away from your job is important. Even a few encouraging words supporting your development and highlighting the contribution of the training can make a huge difference in impact outcomes. In some cases, leaders have the opportunity to attend the same or similar training. This alumni perspective, and hopefully positive endorsement, can mean more impact for the direct-report participants. Imagine getting into an elevator with your leader on a Friday afternoon and as you enter, you

remind him that you are going to training on Monday. He says to you, "Oh yeah—that's right. Oh well, try not to fall asleep. It was really a waste of time. Anyway—have a great weekend and see you on Tuesday." Do you think he's setting you up for success? Do you think you'll go into training focused on the benefits and potential impact? Now consider another manager who says to you, "Oh yeah—that's right. You're really going to enjoy it. I did. It'll help you reach your targets this quarter. Anyway, have a great weekend and let's discuss it on Tuesday. I'd love to hear what you thought about it." Is she setting you up for a more engaging and impactful experience? Which one would you feel better about?

4. *I can "try out" new behaviors or practices on the job without fear of sanctions or negative consequences.* Sometimes, the behaviors and skills taught in training are not consistent with the norms or typical practices that are accepted on the job. For example, a leadership course or training program that encourages constructive confrontation or expressing disagreement with senior leaders may not be easily transferred back to the "real world." It may encourage actions that are viewed by your organization or office culture as too aggressive and confrontational. While all organizations, in theory, want to encourage innovation and create a safe forum for the free exchange of ideas, the reality is there's a long-standing hierarchy to be acknowledged and respected. When training encourages things like "speaking your mind" or "pushing back," you always have to make sure your interpretation of these behaviors, and your intentions to apply them, are filtered through the culture and norms of your organization. Because most employees can't know exactly where to draw the line every time, they will naturally err on the side of caution and not ruffle too many feathers. This

will certainly affect how they apply the learned behaviors and may ultimately dilute the impact of training. While developing some training content in-house can mitigate this factor, employees will still be reticent to apply and adopt any new practices that may not readily be viewed as "productive." They will surely be even less likely to apply those training-related behaviors that clearly violate protocol or that have even the slightest chance of leading to harsher negative consequences.

5. *My coworkers encourage me to "go above and beyond" current levels of performance.* Beyond the support and recognition of leaders, a strong predictor of performance on the job can be the influence and encouragement of peer groups. Rooting for the success of team members and fellow employees can help create on-the-job reinforcements that really drive employee productivity. In fact, because the presence and influence of one's peers is so prevalent and pervasive in most companies, they can sometimes exert even more influence over employees than the leaders. Because of this potential influence, the desired impact of any training and the types of behaviors that are being changed and improved will always be affected by peer pressure. If extremely high performance only gets you a few accolades from your boss, but forces you to sit alone in the lunch room every day, you'll never get as much out of the training as you should. If you make everyone else look bad and contentious glances are always on the menu, you may not last long in that company anyway—no matter how well you perform. Conversely, if your higher performance brings you rock star status and everyone benefits (e.g., team-based incentives) from your productivity improvements, you're going to get more out of any training designed to push those metrics. While most organizations are good at aligning formal and informal incentives, you'd be surprised at how many get it wrong.

6. *I have the time and opportunity to apply these training behaviors on the job.* Despite the highest quality training and all the best intentions, if participants simply don't have the opportunity to apply and practice those training-related behaviors on the job, there's no way they're going to demonstrate impact and ROI. This is why the very early stages of training development and evaluation planning should be aligned. Remember, the training should focus on the behaviors that have the most impact on the most critical business metrics. Simply put, the behaviors must be crucial to doing the job well. In some cases, training will try to ramp people up or place them in a pipeline for their next role. That's fine for career planning, but it makes measuring the impact of the present training almost impossible. For instance, superb presentation skills may be an absolute must for your next role as leader, but if you're spending your whole day right now entering data, there's no way to tell if your public speaking class was effective. You may have gone from a boring speaker to a brilliant orator—but you'll never know until you get up to the podium.

7. *It is clear to me how applying this training will impact the metrics that really matter to my business.* I'm sure by now you're sick of hearing me talk about the link that needs to exist between the Level 3 behaviors and the Level 4 business metrics, but I'm going to tell you one more way it affects your results. Beyond the data linkages that will make your measurement strategy a success, the linkage must also be made in the hearts and minds of the participants. Do the participants who attend the training see a clear and obvious connection between the objectives of the training and the metrics that really drive their business? That is, does the training have face validity? While you've probably already asked this type of question in your Level 1

or 2, it's definitely worth including it again in your Level 6. I say this because you want to check its correlation to Level 3 and 4 scores, but you don't want to have to dig up old Level 1 or 2 scores to do it. Matching these scores for each and every participant would be too time consuming and impractical. It's much easier to throw this question in with the Level 6 transfer factors so you can have all the data on one page to do your correlations. Here you will get a clearer picture of how this factor ultimately predicts behavior change and business impact. Not only should employees see this connection between their behavior and the business metrics, but the metrics must also be those that are most valuable and core to the success of the business.

8. *My leader advocates for my development and wants me to advance in this company.* Although this sounds a lot like supporting a development program and endorsing a particular piece of training (our third factor in the index), there is a clear distinction between the two factors. Supporting a training initiative is a smaller, but more targeted leader behavior while advocating for someone's development and caring about their overall success is a much larger, broader range of behaviors. While supporting a particular training and development program can be a powerful predictor, if that support does not come with a backdrop of overall commitment to an employee's growth and upward mobility, a lot of that perception of support can be lost. In fact, this feeling of overall advocacy and genuine commitment can make employees look for ways to apply the training and grow their skills even if the leader does not come right out and support it. Both layers of encouragement are important when it comes to transferring learning.

9. *I really want to apply the behaviors I learned in training.* The participant's desire to actually apply the training may sound like

(and should be) an automatic assumption we make up front, but in reality this is not always a given. For some of the reasons covered by our other factors (e.g., support, peer pressure, clear link to business) or different ones entirely, not all participants want to apply the training and change their behaviors. While most of the factors we've covered already describe external forces influencing the transfer of learning from training to the job, this one speaks more to the internal, psychological influences that come from within the participant. While many of the external factors can surely influence this psychological state, this may be even more influenced by things like self-efficacy (feeling confident in your ability to apply your learning and be successful), personal resistance to change (not wanting to veer away from how you've always done things), and/or simply an expression of your own long-standing belief that training just doesn't work and is a waste of time. These psychological predispositions set the earliest stage for the transfer of the training. If you're excited, ready, willing, and able to apply the training, your learning will have positive transfer and greater impact. If you're apprehensive, skeptical, and already set in your ways, you'll have far less impact. If you're the old dog that really can't learn new tricks, don't bother going to training.

10. *The behaviors taught in the training are extremely relevant to my specific job role.* The notion that whatever you learn in training can swiftly be turned into everyday efficiencies on the job is critical to transfer and impact. While this is related to one's opportunity to apply the training and making a clear connection to business results, it is more sensitive and effective at honing in on how well all the content of the training matches or overlaps all the behaviors and performance needs

of the employee's role. That is, are they just learning skills and behaviors they need once in a while, or are they practicing tasks they can apply tomorrow. If the totality of the training experience only covers a few of these everyday tasks or is too generic to directly apply, there will be less transfer. If every module, speaker, or bullet point addresses something an employee is currently struggling with, or definitely wants to improve, he/she will get far greater transfer and impact. Any time trainees feel the content was created or customized just for them they will have a more positive reaction and be more likely to change and improve their behaviors.

11. *I will get compensated for my productivity improvements.* Nothing can be more of a motivator for applying what you learned in training and improving your performance than getting a pay raise or promotion. Feeling that you are fairly compensated for your discretionary effort can be extremely powerful at predicting how hard you try to reach your goals. If employees do in fact learn ways to improve their on-the-job behaviors, they will want pay and promotion practices to reflect those higher levels of performance. These are the formal organizational rewards that come far less frequently than the recognition and informal rewards doled out by immediate leaders. If compensation systems and packages don't align with higher performance levels, employees may simply not try to work harder and more efficiently. What this means for training impact is the training can be engaging, relevant, and supported by leaders, but because there's no long- or short-term payoff, it just doesn't get transferred back to the job. For instance, if a sales specialist attends a training program that teaches all the best techniques for closing a sale, but her take-home pay is not based on commission, she may simply never apply any of the new techniques and deliberately keep her sales numbers status quo.

12. *I am committed to the success of this company.* Sometimes an employee is just not excited about seeing an organization grow and compete in the marketplace. In fact, some employees may be more excited about tarnishing its brand and watching it go right down the tubes! Some employees internalize the success of their company and make it their own, while others root for its demise. Wanting to see your company survive and thrive is a good reason to do your part every day and strive to meet organizational goals. Since training is designed to help all employees meet these goals, those who aren't excited (or at least onboard with the goals) will never derive much from training. While motivations and moods may fluctuate, and you may have a small love-hate relationship with your organization, at the end of the day you should want it to succeed. The extent to which you are committed to your organization and its mission statement will affect your commitment to training. If it flies in the face of your own values, ethics, or life philosophy, there's no way you'll be motivated to improve your performance.

While I strongly recommend these 12 items as core to your first iteration, I also encourage you to tweak the wording a bit or add one or two of your own if you suspect you have a unique situation in your organization. Just because these show up the most, doesn't mean they cover every possible scenario. Remember, my research and resultant assessment certainly focuses in on the most powerful and most frequent indicators, but the wording is deliberately broad enough to capture the results of many diverse studies. This makes it universally applicable at the possible expense of some very unique organizational situations. When it comes to diagnosing your own unique climate and creating solutions to "warm" that climate, the devil is almost always in the detail. The more specific your items, the more concise the answers; the more concise the answers, the more targeted your solutions. This tweaking might be as large scale as adding or deleting an item that doesn't fit, or as small as changing a word to reflect the very unique jargon that can exist within any given organization. The important thing to remember here is to just ensure all questions are simple and make sense to your survey-takers. If you decide to add a few exploratory items, I would recommend reviewing your very first waves of Level 3 results. Specifically, the trainees' open-ended (text) examples of successful behavior change. There are often some conspicuous and glaring indicators of what's influencing them in these on-the-job success stories.

Scaling and Scoring Your Climate Assessment

Okay. You know which climate elements you want to include, so now you just have to create a scale for your response options. This should be a six-point scale because you want to make it easier to correlate to your Level 3 scores (which are also a six-point scale). That is, after scoring all your responses, you will ultimately be matching climate item scores (a possible 1–6) to Level 3 scores (another possible 1–6). The actual options should be a scale capturing the extent to which each climate element exists (or should I say perceived to exist) in the employees' immediate work environment. For instance, the question about manager involvement will appear as:

My immediate manager meets with me one-on-one to discuss how I can or have applied the training on the job.					
1	2	3	4	5	6
Strongly disagree	Disagree	Somewhat disagree	Somewhat Agree	Agree	Strongly agree

Now load all the factors and scales into your index. See table 6.2 for a complete Transfer Climate assessment.

Table 6.2 The Transfer Climate Assessment

1. My immediate manager meets with me one-on-one to discuss how I can or have applied the training on the job

1	2	3	4	5	6
Strongly disagree	Disagree	Somewhat disagree	Somewhat agree	Agree	Strongly agree

2. I expect my leader to recognize and reward me for making improvements and applying what I learned in training

1	2	3	4	5	6
Strongly disagree	Disagree	Somewhat disagree	Somewhat agree	Agree	Strongly agree

3. My immediate manager expresses his/her support and endorsement for the training

1	2	3	4	5	6
Strongly disagree	Disagree	Somewhat disagree	Somewhat agree	Agree	Strongly agree

4. I can try out new behaviors or practices on the job without fear of sanctions or negative consequences

1	2	3	4	5	6
Strongly disagree	Disagree	Somewhat disagree	Somewhat agree	Agree	Strongly agree

5. My coworkers encourage me to go above and beyond current levels of performance

1	2	3	4	5	6
Strongly disagree	Disagree	Somewhat disagree	Somewhat agree	Agree	Strongly agree

6. I have the time and opportunity to apply these training behaviors on the job

1	2	3	4	5	6
Strongly disagree	Disagree	Somewhat disagree	Somewhat agree	Agree	Strongly agree

continued

Table 6.2 Continued

7. It's clear to me how applying this training will impact the metrics that really matter to my business

1	2	3	4	5	6
Strongly disagree	Disagree	Somewhat disagree	Somewhat agree	Agree	Strongly agree

8. My immediate manager advocates for my development and wants me to advance in this company

1	2	3	4	5	6
Strongly disagree	Disagree	Somewhat disagree	Somewhat agree	Agree	Strongly agree

9. I really want to apply the knowledge and behaviors I learned in this training

1	2	3	4	5	6
Strongly disagree	Disagree	Somewhat disagree	Somewhat agree	Agree	Strongly agree

10. The behaviors taught in training are extremely relevant to my specific job role

1	2	3	4	5	6
Strongly disagree	Disagree	Somewhat disagree	Somewhat agree	Agree	Strongly agree

11. I will get compensated for my productivity improvements

1	2	3	4	5	6
Strongly disagree	Disagree	Somewhat disagree	Somewhat agree	Agree	Strongly agree

12. I am committed to the success of this company.

1	2	3	4	5	6
Strongly disagree	Disagree	Somewhat disagree	Somewhat agree	Agree	Strongly agree

Transfer Climate Assessment—done. How and when do you administer it? Well here comes some more great news—you simply attach your index to the Level 3 and Level 4 questionnaire that already goes out to participants three months post training. That's right—Once you develop your best first draft, the index then simply gets added (as a subset of new questions) to your current post-training evaluation. *Yes—we can gather data for our Levels 3, 4, 5, and 6 from the same survey. I can't make it any simpler than that.*

Analyzing and Reporting your Level 6 Results

Once you have your data in hand, there are two ways to analyze and report your Level 6 results: correlation and critical incidence For either technique you will simply be comparing the scores on your climate question to overall Level 3 behavior change. I would strongly recommend presenting both approaches. The correlation establishes a scientific and statistical link between training application and climate, and the critical incidence graphically shows your audience just how dramatic this effect can be. The first will be a stiff jab to get their attention and the second will be the power punch to drive the point home.

Correlation

Are the employees that are reporting the greatest improvements in behavior and business results also scoring higher on your climate questions? Are the ones who were not affected by the training scoring lower on those same climate questions? Some will correlate, some will not. The higher your correlation for each factor, the stronger the climate factor.

To calculate the correlation coefficient for each factor, you will be comparing the scores of your climate questions to the scores on your Level 3 questions. That is, you look at how each participant responded to *each climate question* in your index and match or correlate that number (possible 1–6) to each participant's *aggregate Level 3 results* (possible 1–6). The correlation analysis used here can be done using any of the statistical softwares available (SPSS, SAS, etc.). The analysis will actually calculate a correlation coefficient for each of the transfer climate elements included in your assessment; the higher the number, the stronger the relationship.

So what kind of numbers are we talking about? Well, the closer your correlation gets to a 1.0, the more powerful the relationship between your two variables. A value of 1.0 is the maximum and highest correlation you can achieve, but even in the most controlled and perfectly designed experiments a value of 1.0 is almost always unattainable. In this example, it would mean that once you get a participant's score on his/her transfer climate, you could then perfectly predict (with 100 percent accuracy) exactly what level of behavior change they will demonstrate on the job. Wouldn't that be something! A perfect correlation of 1.0 would also mean that the transfer climate element you are analyzing is the *only* thing that effects a participant's behavior change. With all the other possible environmental confounds, individual differences, and everyday nuances in our work life, you can see why this would be impossible.

So what's a good number? The good news about all this stat stuff is that you really don't need to get anywhere close to that perfect 1.0. All you have to do is show a "significant" relationship between a climate element and behavior change and you've already made an incredible contribution to the business. Depending on your data, even a correlation of .20 or .30 can be statistically significant and powerful enough to impress your business leaders. Remember, this literally means that you have identified a factor in employees' work environments that makes training "more likely" to succeed. That is, of all the things that can help or hinder the impact of training, you have just uncovered a significant one that makes it more effective. Doesn't that sound like a piece of information business leaders would want to get their hands on? After all, knowing this type of information could potentially mean either wasting or optimizing their training dollars.

Once you have a correlation coefficient for each of the items in your index, just create a table that lists all the climate elements along with their correlation values. From this table, just start ranking your climate factors according to how highly they correlate. From the original list of *twelve* factors in your index, you want to reveal the mightiest and most predictive of the bunch. Finally, take your highest ranking *top three* and they become your *critical transfer climate factors. They become your bridge's pillars! The three things you absolutely need to address and build into your training design in the future.* This is how you maximize transfer. This is how you maximize ROI! See figure 6.1 showing the top three climate factors I found in one of my own studies.

WHAT ARE YOUR TOP 3?

Which transfer climate factors are your strongest?

Top 3 Correlations:

I have one on one meetings with my leader to discuss how I can apply this training on my job	.58*
My leader supports my training and believes it has a positive impact on my performance	.49*
I believe I will be recognized and rewarded for improving my behaviors and performance	.41*

* Correlation Analysis. N=3208, p<.05

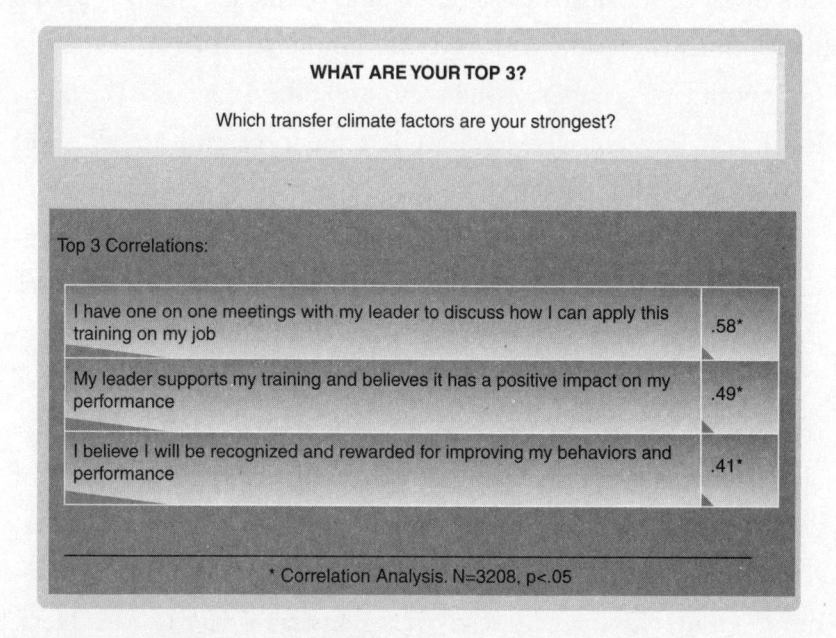

Figure 6.1 Three "make or break" climate factors.

Critical Incidence

While the correlation analysis is great for *proving* your factors are important, the critical incidence analysis is great at *showing* your factors are important. That is, it takes a statistical relationship (your correlation coefficient) and illustrates what that really means and how it plays out within your training population. It literally shows how the presence or absence of your factors can lead to very disparate outcomes. As we have already done for previous levels, we are separating our sample into two "critical" groups—the participants who had "high improvement" in their behaviors (Group A) and the participants who showed "no improvement" (Group B). Remember, these same two groups were captured with your Level 3. I told you they would come in handy! Once separated, you then simply compare how each of these two groups answered your transfer climate questions. Are there any significant and conspicuous differences in the way these two groups answer each of your climate items? For instance, if most of the "high improvement" group is saying their immediate leader endorsed the training, and most of the "no improvement" group is saying their leader didn't endorse the training, it certainly looks like leader endorsement is a strong predictor of improvement and impact.

Using the same study and factors identified in figure 6.1, figure 6.2 shows you a critical incidence analysis. Here, you can see that there were very huge differences in the way the two groups were responding to the top three climate factors. For instance, if you take the first factor (having one-on-one conversations with your leader about how to apply the training) you will see that 72 percent of employees in the "high improvement" were having these conversations with their leaders, while only 17 percent of the "no improvement" group had these same conversations with their leaders. Here,

How Do We Maximize Impact? • 141

Level 6
HOW DO CLIMATE FACTORS AFFECT IMPROVEMENT AND IMPACT?
Critical Incidence Analysis

[Bar chart showing three Transfer Climate Factors comparing No Improvement Group (gray) vs. High Improvement Group (black):
- Has conversations with leader about how to apply training: 17% / 72%
- Has a leader who endorses training: 31% / 82%
- Expects to be rewarded for improved behaviors: 33% / 75%

Callouts: "75% of employees in the high improvement group expect to be rewarded when they apply the training" and "33% of employees in the no improvement group expect to be rewarded when they apply the training"]

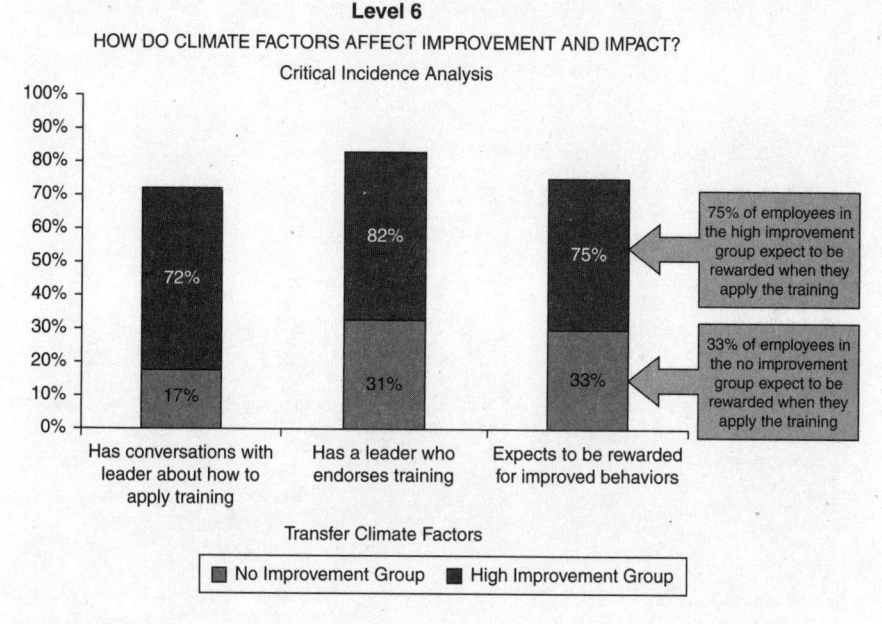

Figure 6.2 How do your top three factors discriminate between levels of impact?

you can conclude that having a supportive leader who has these critical conversations is predicting training impact.

This figure shows how all three factors were present and pervasive for the "high improvement" group, while they were all significantly lower for the "no improvement" group.

Summing Up Your Level 6

Okay. You gave them the old one-two punch with your correlation and critical incidence analysis and now you're ready for the knockout! Here, you just wrap up all your results into one irrefutable headline—"Your Climate Predicts Your ROI." Spell it out for them. In one slide, show them that the climate elements cause the behavior change, the behavior change causes your business impact, and your business impact leads to bottom-line returns. See an example in figure 6.3.

TRANSFER CLIMATE DRIVES IMPACT

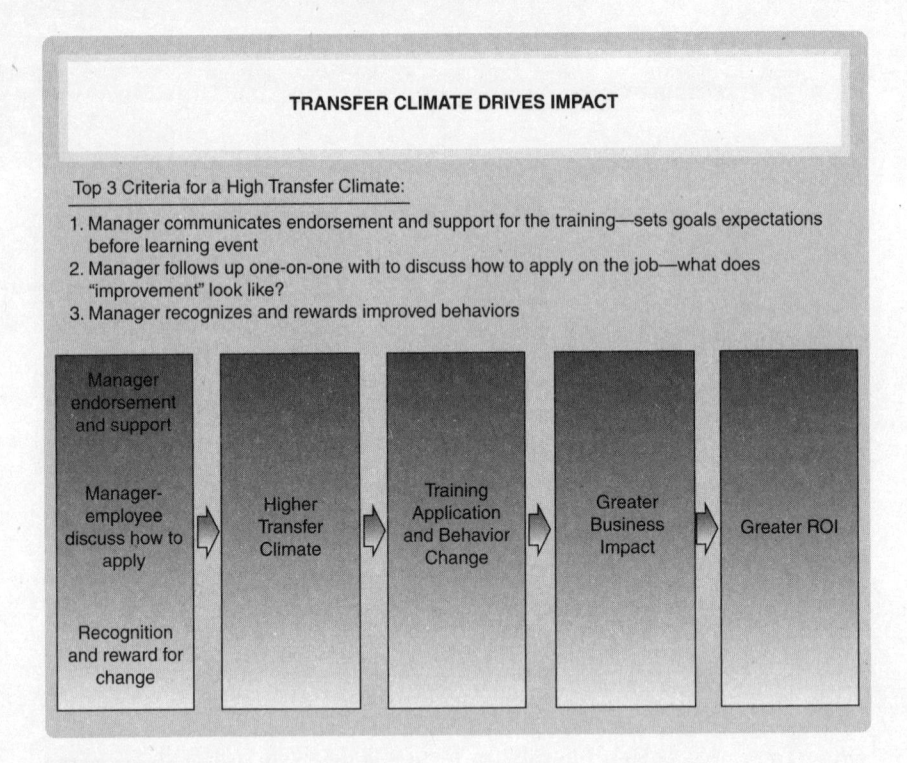

Top 3 Criteria for a High Transfer Climate:
1. Manager communicates endorsement and support for the training—sets goals expectations before learning event
2. Manager follows up one-on-one with to discuss how to apply on the job—what does "improvement" look like?
3. Manager recognizes and rewards improved behaviors

Manager endorsement and support
Manager-employee discuss how to apply
Recognition and reward for change
⇒ Higher Transfer Climate
⇒ Training Application and Behavior Change
⇒ Greater Business Impact
⇒ Greater ROI

Figure 6.3 Better climate = greater ROI.

Okay. What would an organization do with these results? Well, for this particular study you will notice that my three top criteria for a high transfer climate all happen to fall squarely on the shoulders of each participant's immediate leader or supervisor. That made it glaringly obvious to the client organization that before they put any more time and money into new training, they should first make a much cheaper and infinitely more valuable investment into changing their climate. More specifically, teach their leaders what to do for participants before, during, and after the training event. They successfully addressed just those top three factors and "warmed" their climate just a little. Months later they saw more impact from training and ultimately more bountiful returns on their training dollars.

Okay. Now you've got your own factors in your own organization. You've presented your data and convinced your audience with some very compelling evidence that these specific aspects of the employees' climate need to be improved in order to get the most out of their training dollars. Now it's time to act. It's time to build your own solution that affects your top three factors and changes your climate. *It's time to finish building your bridge.*

Finish Building Your Bridge

Recently, I was presenting my training evaluation results for a huge global financial corporation. All of the bigwigs were there including the president of human resources. The training being assessed was a flagship leadership program for thousands of leaders across the organization. As I moved through my slides and reported on each progressive level of evaluation, I could feel the momentum and excitement building in the room. This type of reporting on Levels 3, 4, and 5 had never been done before. Not only that, but it was certainly the first time they would be hearing about a Level 6. I showed them some significant behavior change and told them a wonderful story of business impact and ROI. Then I told them about the critical climate factors that surfaced as a result of all this research. I told them about the Level 6 factors that were really driving impact when the trainees got back to their everyday jobs. The audience was truly engaged.

Just as I finished speaking, I heard a piercing question shouted from the audience—"So what are we doing about our climate?" Of course I realized instantly the question was coming from the president. What *are* we really doing about it? As any great leader would do, this one immediately shifted from hearing about the great results to wanting to improve those same results. With many different employees and leaders going through the training every week, he wanted to boost the transfer climate and build solutions as soon as possible. He wanted to finish building that bridge.

While I fumbled around referring to a few solutions that were previously brainstormed and barely in the works, I realized that my response was far from adequate. As groundbreaking and insightful as all my results were, I had to conclude my presentation on a very anticlimactic lull because of this pointed and very legitimate last question. It was clear that great research and great results don't add up to much unless you are able to act on them. And these were certainly not the types of findings business leaders could afford to put on the back burner for long. I promised myself and my audience that I would follow-up and return with a "concrete" answer to that question. I promised them a *bridge*.

I tell you this story for two reasons: The first is because I want you to feel the urgency and be prepared for the spotlight your results might create. A great evaluation strategy doesn't end with post-training results. It provides organizations with data to learn, improve, and shape future training strategies. The second reason is I want to use this real-life example to show you how easy building this last part of your bridge can be. Here's how we did it.

The Solution

Our Level 6 research surfaced three critical transfer factors:

1. Leader endorsement of training
2. One-on-one meetings with leader to discuss how training would impact the job
3. Expectation of recognition and reward for improvements

Using these as our targets, our next step was to build a powerful tool and process to integrate them into our training design and really bring them to life.

For the *first factor* (leader endorsement) we knew it was important to deliver these positive words about the training even before the event took place. Here, we told each immediate manager to meet with his/her participants at least once *before* the training to talk about the benefits and get them excited about its potential impact.

For the *second factor* (ongoing meetings to discuss how to apply) we knew this should happen once before the event (to set expectations) and then on a regular basis (weekly) for at least the first three months after the training. In these conversations, we wanted them to cover four things:

1. Choose the behaviors from the training that were most important and relevant to their jobs.
2. Define how these new or improved behaviors will affect their job performance.
3. Firmly agree on what improvement would "look like" over the next three months.
4. Record and monitor these improvements over time.

For the *third factor* (expecting to be rewarded for change) we knew we wanted to make these "recorded" improvements easily transferable over to a middle or year-end performance appraisal. Here, since all employees were already rated on certain key leadership behaviors and had also historically struggled to cite examples, we encouraged both participant and leader to cut and paste their training-related examples of improvement (if applicable) into their middle and year-end rating forms.

After all was said and done, we ended up building a simple impact and sustainability tool we called a TIP (Target Impact Plan). This was just a simple "contract" that spelled out what participants and leaders should do before and after training. This included a one-page agreement between the participant and leader to ensure expectations about improvement on the job were mutually recognized and acknowledged. In a nutshell, the participant and his/her immediate manager agree on the behaviors they want to improve and decide what that improvement would actually look like three months down the road. After the training they use a portion of their already scheduled one-on-ones to highlight and capture real examples of that positive change. See figure 6.4 for a summary of the target impact plan process. While the entire process took almost *no* "extra" energy from either party, it became clear that a few small, yet deliberate and prescriptive actions along the way could make a big difference and yield significant returns for the business.

Follow-up research testing the value of this TIP showed that for those participants using the tool, there were significant improvements in their climate scores, significantly higher levels of behavior change, and significantly higher productivity jumps over the three months that followed the training event. In fact, the participants using TIP to foster the right climate had productivity increases that were 75 percent higher than a control group that did not use TIP. See figure 6.5 for results.

In a nutshell, we created a strong bridge. And beyond presenting the solution and results to our internal business leaders, our process and findings were also published as L&D best practices in the Corporate Executive Board later that year.

The Power of Climate

To give you another example of how powerful this transfer climate can be and how it helped shape training investments, I was once evaluating the effectiveness and impact of web-based versus instructor-led training. Here, using my Level 1–6 evaluation approach, I tested which training delivery mode had more impact—a self-directed web-based delivery or an instructor-led, classroom event.

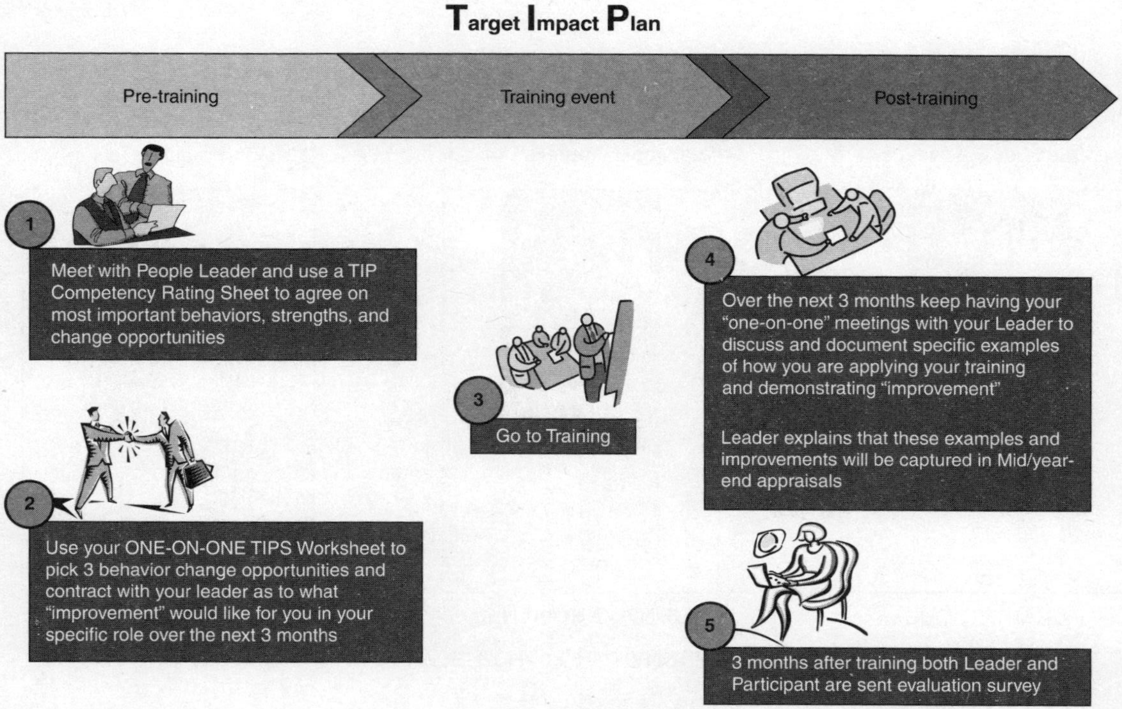

Target Impact Plan

Pre-training | **Training event** | **Post-training**

1. Meet with People Leader and use a TIP Competency Rating Sheet to agree on most important behaviors, strengths, and change opportunities

2. Use your ONE-ON-ONE TIPS Worksheet to pick 3 behavior change opportunities and contract with your leader as to what "improvement" would like for you in your specific role over the next 3 months

3. Go to Training

4. Over the next 3 months keep having your "one-on-one" meetings with your Leader to discuss and document specific examples of how you are applying your training and demonstrating "improvement"

Leader explains that these examples and improvements will be captured in Mid/year-end appraisals

5. 3 months after training both Leader and Participant are sent evaluation survey

Figure 6.4 Target Impact Plan.

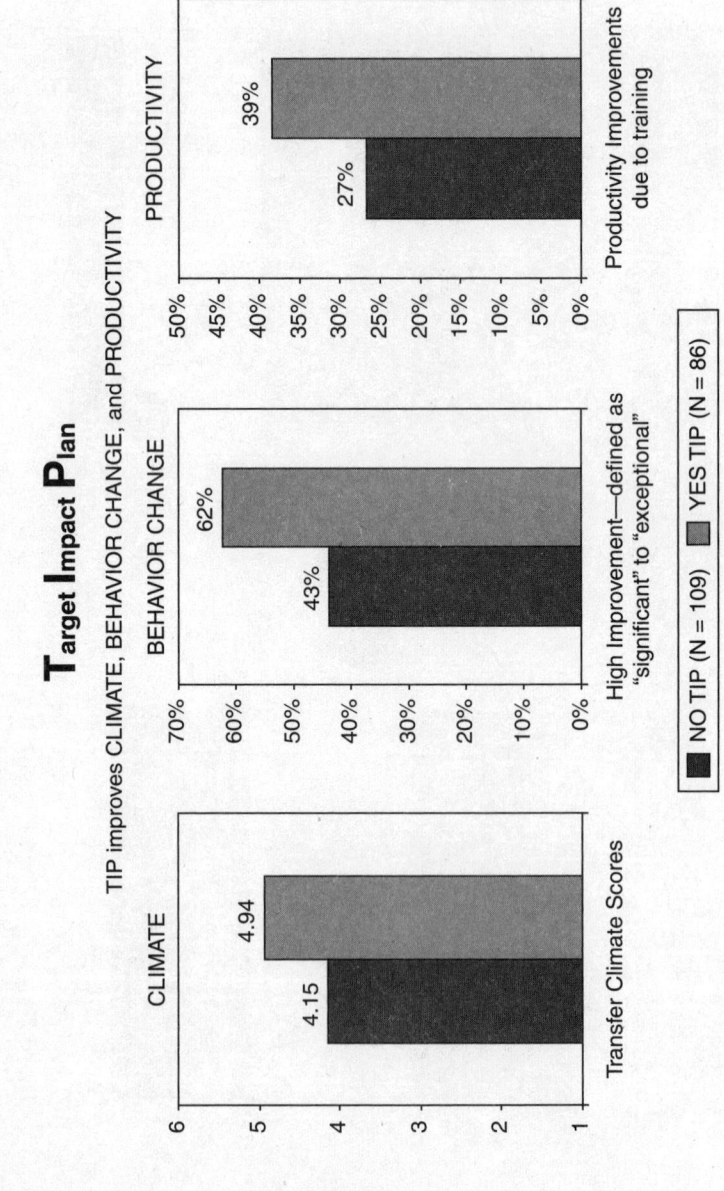

Figure 6.5 Impact of TIP.

Additionally, I tested if there was any difference in effectiveness between the one-day versus the two-day instructor-led option.

In a nutshell, I found that the most powerful predictor of effectiveness was not the delivery mode or the length of the training, but rather the climate participants were returning to after the training. This literally meant that the ultimate impact had less to do with how the trainee received the training (web vs. classroom) or length of training (one vs. two days), and far more to do with their immediate work environment back on the job.

The implications of these findings were huge. This meant that a far less expensive and less time-intensive web-based training program can be just as powerful as an instructor-led program as long as you improve the climate. And why spend more time and money on a two-day training program when a one-day experience with a powerful support climate can be just as effective?

Based on these findings, a "blended" learning approach was developed. This included components like leader-led "kick-offs," "wrap-ups," and consistent follow-up conversations built right into to the participant experience. In fact, a follow-up study that compared all three modes of delivery (ILT vs. WBT vs. blended) found that on average this blended approach had significantly greater transfer climate scores and had almost *75 percent higher ROI* than either the instructor-led or web-based delivery modes alone!

The above results send a powerful message: Before spending a tremendous amount of time and money on content and delivery, organizations should first make a much smaller and *smarter* investment to ensure their climate is right. Understanding and making transfer climates a priority in any training strategy will help organizations achieve the greatest returns and drive the highest possible ROI for their initiatives. This is how you smoothly and effectively move your participants from training event to maximum business impact. This is how you finish building your bridge.

Summary

When I started this book, I told you about a bridge. This bridge connects your training (point of origin) to bottom-line business performance (your destination). It begins with an engaging training experience (Level 1). That training leads to new learning (Level 2). That learning leads to behavior change (Level 3). That behavior change leads to business impact (Level 4). That business impact should be big enough to justify and exceed all training costs (Level 5). These are the stepping stones and critical linkages of your bridge. And all around this bridge is your climate. Do you have the foundation and support pillars to uphold your bridge and keep it strong? Will it be strong enough to withstand all the "inclement" conditions that can knock your trainees off their path and over the side into the cold, dark waters below? And beyond the environmental conditions that frustrate and hinder employees, what about those same crucial climate elements that actually maximize impact and boost the ROI of all your training programs? Evaluating the factors that can strengthen, weaken, or even make or break your bridge is your Level 6. See all six levels labeled in figure S.1.

The one thing you'll need to do at every step in building this bridge is *measure*. Without a solid evaluation strategy to measure the

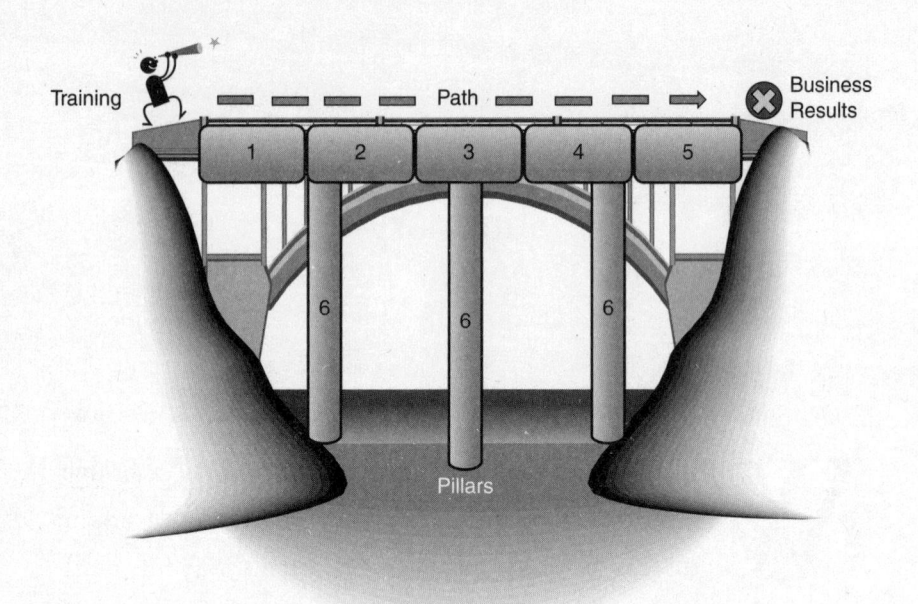

Figure S.1 The bridge.

strength of all these elements that connect and fortify your bridge, you'll never truly be able to tell whether your training has an impact on the bottom line. You'll also never know why and where the journey fails. Without evaluation and measurement you won't even know if your bridge is pointed in the right direction.

Throughout this book I've tried to give you the tools and insights to build your own sturdy bridge and evaluate the training initiatives in your own organizations. My hope is that what seemed before like a daunting and overwhelming venture is now something you are absolutely confident with and ready to jump into. I've armed you with:

- The core questions to cover Levels 1 and 2
- The core questions and templates to develop your own Level 3
- A completely new process and formula to simplify and truly isolate your Level 4

- A quick and simple way to calculate your Level 5
- A new and groundbreaking Level 6 to quantitatively measure the most significant predictor of training impact—Transfer Climate

And the greatest news of all is you can bring all these questions together and collect all the raw data you need using two simple surveys. The first one covers Levels 1 and 2 and is administered right after training. The second covers Level 3, 4, and 6, and is administered three months (may vary) after the training ends. Level 5 data are actually created by just monetizing the Level 4 data you already have. These monetary "benefits" therefore do not have to be collected directly from respondents. See both assessments in what follows.

Post-training Evaluation Covering Levels 1 and 2

Table S.1 Measurement process, Levels 1 and 2

Levels 1 and 2		
Were you engaged by the subject and content of the training? If no, why not?	YES	NO
Are you satisfied with the way the training was delivered? If no, why not?	YES	NO
Are you satisfied with the facilitator? If no, why not?	YES	NO
What was the best part of the experience?		
What was the worst part of the experience?		
Did you gain new knowledge and/or skills from this training? If no, why not?	YES	NO
What was your one biggest takeaway from this training?		
Was the learning important to your role? If no, why not?	YES	NO
Do you intend to apply and use it on the job?	YES	NO
Overall, are you satisfied with the training?	YES	NO
Would you recommend this training to colleagues? Any other comments?	YES	NO

Post-training Evaluation Covering Levels 3–6

Table S.2 Measurement process, Levels 3–6

Level 3

Below is a list of key leader behaviors. For each, describe the level of improvement you've achieved (if any) as a result of applying what you learned in training....

1. **Build effective development plans with direct reports**

1	2	3	4	5	6
Got worse	No improvement	Little improvement	Some improvement	Significant improvement	Exceptional improvement

2. **Another key leader behavior goes here....**

1	2	3	4	5	6
Got worse	No improvement	Little improvement	Some improvement	Significant improvement	Exceptional improvement

3. **Another key leader behavior goes here....**

1	2	3	4	5	6
Got worse	No improvement	Little improvement	Some improvement	Significant improvement	Exceptional improvement

4. **Another key leader behavior goes here....**

1	2	3	4	5	6
Got worse	No improvement	Little improvement	Some improvement	Significant improvement	Exceptional improvement

5. **Another key leader behavior goes here....**

1	2	3	4	5	6
Got worse	No improvement	Little improvement	Some improvement	Significant improvement	Exceptional improvement

6. **Another key leader behavior goes here....**

1	2	3	4	5	6
Got worse	No improvement	Little improvement	Some improvement	Significant improvement	Exceptional improvement

7. Please give an example of your most improved behavior(s) on the job…

Level 4

8. How is your productivity primarily measured? (Drop Down)

Approximately how much has this metric increased for you (if any) over the past three months?
2% 5% 7% 10% 12% 15% 20% 25% 30%… over 100%

Please give a specific example of how you improved business performance…

continued

Table S.2 Continued

Level 6

To what extent do you agree or disagree with the following:

1. My immediate manager meets with me one-on-one to discuss how I can or have applied the training on the job

1	2	3	4	5	6
Strongly disagree	Disagree	Somewhat disagree	Somewhat agree	Agree	Strongly agree

2. I expect my leader to recognize and reward me for making improvements and applying what I learned in training

1	2	3	4	5	6
Strongly disagree	Disagree	Somewhat disagree	Somewhat agree	Agree	Strongly agree

3. My immediate manager expresses his/her support and endorsement for the training

1	2	3	4	5	6
Strongly disagree	Disagree	Somewhat disagree	Somewhat agree	Agree	Strongly agree

4. I can try out new behaviors or practices on the job without fear of sanctions or negative consequences

1	2	3	4	5	6
Strongly disagree	Disagree	Somewhat disagree	Somewhat agree	Agree	Strongly agree

5. My coworkers encourage me to go above and beyond current levels of performance

1	2	3	4	5	6
Strongly disagree	Disagree	Somewhat disagree	Somewhat agree	Agree	Strongly agree

6. I have the time and opportunity to apply these training behaviors on the job

1	2	3	4	5	6
Strongly disagree	Disagree	Somewhat disagree	Somewhat agree	Agree	Strongly agree

7. It's clear to me how applying this training will impact the metrics that really matter to my business

1	2	3	4	5	6
Strongly disagree	Disagree	Somewhat disagree	Somewhat agree	Agree	Strongly agree

8. My immediate manager advocates for my development and wants me to advance in this company

1	2	3	4	5	6
Strongly disagree	Disagree	Somewhat disagree	Somewhat agree	Agree	Strongly agree

9. I really want to apply the knowledge and behaviors I learned in this training

1	2	3	4	5	6
Strongly disagree	Disagree	Somewhat disagree	Somewhat agree	Agree	Strongly agree

10. The behaviors taught in training are extremely relevant to my specific job role

1	2	3	4	5	6
Strongly disagree	Disagree	Somewhat disagree	Somewhat agree	Agree	Strongly agree

11. I will get compensated for my productivity improvements

1	2	3	4	5	6
Strongly disagree	Disagree	Somewhat disagree	Somewhat agree	Agree	Strongly agree

12. I am committed to the success of this company

1	2	3	4	5	6
Strongly disagree	Disagree	Somewhat disagree	Somewhat agree	Agree	Strongly agree

Measuring Impact and Return on Investment

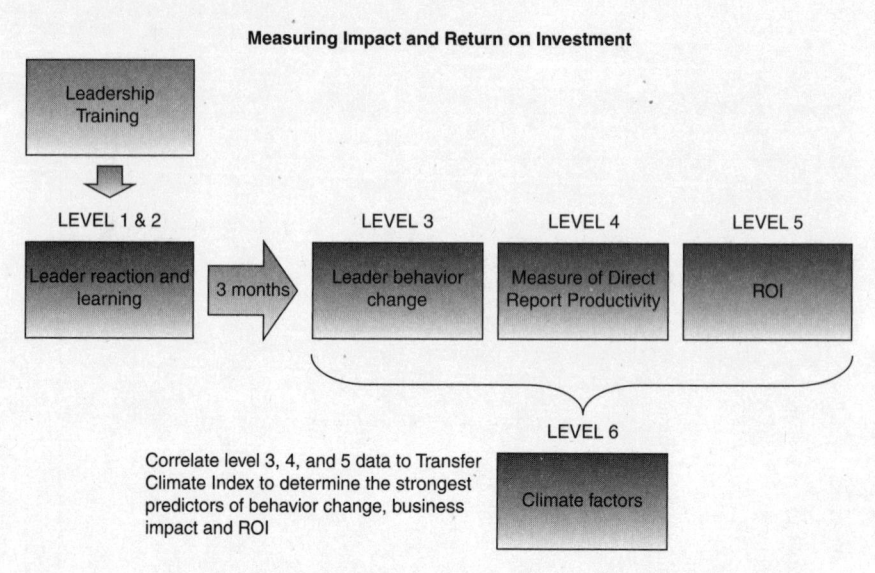

Figure S.2 The measurement process.

These two assessments combined should take your participants and any other raters no more than 15–20 minutes. Of course, to build the chain of impact you will have to do some analysis and story-building behind the scenes, but the time you are asking from your businesses and employees is minimal. Imagine, within just a few months, you can go from not measuring and evaluating training at all to having a complete Level 1–6 evaluation strategy. See sample measurement strategy in figure S.2.

Using the sample slides and examples I've shown you throughout this book, you should now be able to analyze and present all your own results for each of these levels. If you have to, you can even break all six levels down to a one-page, at-a-glance summary slide for your business leaders who might just want the headlines. See a summary snapshot in figure S.3.

As part of this simple, but comprehensive strategy, I also emphasized throughout this book the importance of adding a Level 6—Transfer Climate analysis to your traditional five levels of evaluation. This new level of measurement helps you uncover the real

Level 1–6 Evaluation Results

Level 1	**93%** of participants were engaged and satisfied
Level 2	**91%** of participants acquired new knowledge that helped them do their job better
Level 3	The behaviors most impacted by this training were: 1. Identify and remove employees' obstacles to better performance 2. Have more frequent coaching conversations with direct reports 3. Give more frequent and positive feedback **95%** of participants demonstrated improvements in these key leader behaviors **54%** demonstrated significant to exceptional improvement **86%** of their direct reports observed improvement in these key leadership behaviors **59%** observed significant to exceptional improvement in their leaders
Level 4	Direct reports of these trainees were significantly affected by these improved leader behaviors. There was an average of **8%** increase in productivity (sales revenue) directly attributable to the training—Total Effect Size.
Level 5	The Return on Investment (ROI) per participant was **450%**.
Level 6	The Top 3 Climate Factors that are maximizing the impact of this training are: 1. **Participant's leaders explicitly support and endorse the training** 2. **Participant's leaders have regular one-on-one follow-up conversations about how to apply the training on the job** 3. **Participants feel they will be recognized or rewarded for any behavior changes they make**

Figure S.3 Final takeaways.

reasons why the training works or doesn't work. It illuminates the critical climate factors back on the job that help create such incredible impact for some employees, while for others, the training becomes a disappointing waste of time and resources. Through such analysis, you'll not only be able to identify the critical drivers of impact, but more importantly you'll be able to create simple, inexpensive solutions to target these climate factors and vastly increase the ROI of your training in the future.

As evidenced in my research, improving these transfer factors and making positive climate changes can be even more critical to impact than the actual training itself. Of course you want to choose a great training program, but even the greatest content can be ineffective if you don't focus very deliberately and precisely on your transfer climate. Once you have the right climate, any training you plug in and implement will be able to achieve its maximum potential for business impact and ROI. These climate factors are the support pillars that hold up your bridge. Without them, your bridge crumbles and trainees never make it to their destination. Without them in place, any training initiative can quickly amount to a colossal waste of time and money. Don't spend another penny on training until you build your bridge.

Conclusion

Measuring the impact of your training is no longer a nice-to-have. It's an absolute business imperative. Measurement not only defines the chain of impact at every level, but actually makes that impact happen. It creates and builds the proverbial "bridge" between a training event and its ultimate ROI. By simply defining how learning leads to employee behavior change and how that employee behavior change leads to business results, your measurement strategy actually brings the story of impact to life. It describes in detail the employee's journey from training event to business results and allows you to identify all the factors along the way that can either facilitate or block them from reaching their destination. By defining and measuring each step in this journey, you are in essence holding the hands of participants and helping them traverse this treacherous path to bottom-line impact. Simply put, *measuring the impact of your training will maximize the impact of your training.*

Considering all the steps and studies I've shown you in this book, you should now be able to go back to your business leaders and tell them not only whether training is "working" or not (Level 1–5), but also how to make that very same training more effective in the future (Level 6). Without a full and comprehensive measurement strategy that accounts for environmental influences, you will never truly understand how training influences employee behaviors and how those behaviors impact the bottom line. And if you don't understand how employees impact the bottom line, you'll never be able to improve that bottom line. You will find yourself delivering training and then simply hoping that it has an impact on the business somewhere down the road. And any successful leader in any industry will tell you that just hoping for anything somewhere down the road, especially in business, is a losing proposition.

With organizations all over the world spending billions of dollars a year on training, and the success of their businesses actually depending on the effectiveness of that training, it's no wonder they are all swiftly realizing how critical it is to measure training impact. In this economy (or any economy for that matter), it's not alright to spend that much money and have nothing to show for it. Whether you are looking to keep your current training, bring in new training, create your own training, or completely change the way you deliver training, the one and only way to make these decisions and support your entire training strategy is to measure impact. Whether your budget is shrinking or growing, evaluating your initiatives (Level 1–6) is the key to delivering the highest impact training in the most cost-effective way.

The reason why the training industry has struggled so long to prove its worth is because it has rarely been shown how to prove its worth. The "costs" are always so real and tangible, while the "benefits" have historically been anecdotal and ill-defined. Sure, we know the training industry is alive and well, and will only grow stronger, as employees need to have even richer, more diverse, and adaptive skill sets. But the real question is—Can't we do better? If we know measuring the impact of training creates more impact, shouldn't this be one of our most urgent priorities. Shouldn't we be able to show our stakeholders how they can take those same training dollars and improve the impact of a training event the second time around?

Shouldn't we at long last be able to show our business leaders that the benefits of training can far outweigh the costs? If we don't start defining these critical benefits and showing the value we can bring as experts in our field, why should we ever get that coveted seat at the C-table? And believe me, if you measure training and put some real bottom-line numbers in front of your stakeholders, they'll not only believe you, but they'll thank you for it. And all it takes is a small investment in measurement up front. Talk about an ROI.

As training professionals, we put such incredible resources into trying to find the most "effective" training solution *out there*, when the first thing we need to fix is what's *in here*—our internal training climate. We spend so much time and money looking for the next best thing and dreaming up the most creative ways to deliver it that the true predictors of success and impact slip right through our fingers. Instead of being so quick to look for new training or different training, our first and hardest look should be at our current training and the simple climate factors that we can fix right now. Don't get me wrong, I'm all for new training and *lots of it*, but don't you want to make sure you're getting the most out of anything you buy or build? And with employees at all levels of the organization being able to implement and effect these positive climate changes, the importance and urgency to create a great climate should swiftly move to the forefront of any training strategy. Especially at times when you need to stretch that training budget, measuring your levels and capitalizing on these factors can help you deliver your initiatives in a way that squeezes every last penny out of those precious training dollars. As I said in the introduction and as I've intimated throughout this book: Don't waste another penny on training until you build your bridge.

CASE STUDY 1

Measuring the Impact of Leadership Training

I dread getting up in the morning and facing my leader. I don't understand how I got stuck with such a @#$%—Help!

She's so awesome—I am truly blessed!

These are two actual comments that I received from two employees describing their leaders in this study. I immediately asked myself—How can these employees be equally productive on the job? While these extreme cases certainly don't represent the state of affairs for all leaders and their direct reports in the organization, they do highlight and reinforce how important it is to have a good leader doing the right things to motivate you every day. Across any large organization, on any given day, there are thousands of employees being influenced in big ways by little things their leader does or says throughout the day. Consequently, any change or improvement in these leaders can have a profound and resounding effect on employees' performance and productivity. This is what was measured in this study.

For this case study, we looked at the direct effects of a leadership training program across the organization. More specifically, we looked at how the training improved key leadership behaviors and then how those leadership behaviors improved the productivity of direct reports. When it comes to measuring the powerful effects of training, good ROI studies are hard to come by. When it comes to measuring the powerful effects of leadership training, the numbers get even more dismal and the impact studies just about disappear. This study not only measures the results of a leadership program from Level 1 (Reaction) to Level 5 (Return on Investment), but also introduces a Level 6 (Transfer Climate), which identifies the environmental factors and leading "indicators" that either help or hinder a learner from applying their new knowledge and skills back on the job.

The Company

The company was a Fortune 100 global organization with more than 50,000 employees in over 45 countries. As a financial company in the service industry, this organization realized that in order to thrive in its market it needed to create a customer experience that would be unparalleled by its competitors. As part of this vision, the overall HR talent strategy included a laser-sharp focus on people leadership. That is, they wanted to make sure all their employees were maximally inspired, engaged, and motivated by their immediate managers. They wanted to increase overall leadership capability and effectiveness in key areas and equip their 8,000+ people leaders with the skills to truly motivate and drive the results of their employees.

A key population within the target group and our sample for this particular study (N = 1,974) were front-line managers. One of the most critical roles within any sales or service function is the front-line manager or team leader. These leaders typically work right in the organization's sales/call centers and are responsible for coaching and

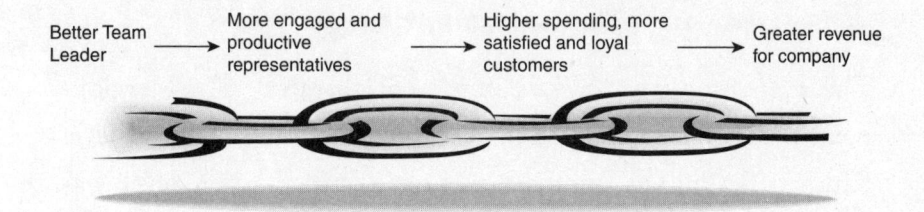

Better Team Leader → More engaged and productive representatives → Higher spending, more satisfied and loyal customers → Greater revenue for company

Figure CS1.1 The good leader profit chain.

supporting the front-line, customer-facing employees who can quite literally make or break relationships with customers every day. These customer-facing employees hold the key to establishing and building the company's brand and reputation every time they pick up the phone or engage a customer. And no one influences them more directly and profoundly than their immediate leaders. Operating on the principles of what I call the "good leader profit chain" (simply stated: Good leader = happy employees = happy customers = happy shareholders), these people leaders were meant to impact the business bottom line by increasing the engagement and productivity of all their immediate direct reports (see figure CS1.1).

The Training

The flagship leader training program came from a renowned vendor in the training industry and was chosen because of its ability to target specific leadership competencies and tasks, while remaining flexible enough to translate across an incredibly diverse leader population. It provided a model whereby leaders partner with direct reports, diagnose their specific needs, and develop unique action plans for each employee. While the training program was chosen and implemented before I got there, the size of the target population and the staggering of the rollout over the following year allowed ample opportunity to align my evaluation strategy with the training objectives.

The Evaluation Strategy

The evaluation and overall impact of the leadership development efforts were measured in part using the traditional five-level Kirkpatrick/Phillips approach. Then, a critical sixth level was added to identify the environmental factors that can profoundly influence the impact of the training back on the job (see table CS1.1 for description of evaluation level and measurement approach).

The first thing we had to do to implement this evaluation strategy, and ensure a successful measurement approach, was align the goals and desired outcomes of the organization with the objectives and outcomes of the training program. This meant creating a chain of impact, blueprint, or "bridge" between the training event and the desired business results. We started at the destination and worked our way backwards from the business results (Level 4) to the on-the-job behaviors (Level 3) that employees needed to improve in order

Table CS1.1 Six Levels of evaluation

Measurement	Method of evaluation
Level 1: Reaction	Learner responds to different components of the training experience. Provides overall description of satisfaction with training
Level 2: Knowledge	Learner rates/describes new knowledge and skills acquired as a result of the training
Level 3: Behavior	Learner and direct reports rate observed improvement in specific leadership skills
Level 4: Impact	Learner and direct reports identify primary business metrics and assessment measures improved productivity of direct reports
Level 5: ROI	Benefit versus cost analysis based on increase in productivity of direct reports over three months. Benefits are monetized and compared to overall cost of training program
Level 6: Transfer Climate	Assesses factors in participant's work environment (transfer climate) that help or hinder the transfer of learning back to the job. Measures how these factors influence and predict training impact and outcomes

to achieve those results. Then we had to determine which training objectives (Level 2) would impact or overlap those behaviors the most. In order to start building our bridge, we needed to know the following: Which metrics had to improve? Which behaviors would improve those metrics? And what did the participants need to learn in training to make all this happen?

For Level 4, because this was a leadership program, we knew we had to look at the productivity levels of the participants' direct reports. That is, what were the metrics that were really driving the success of their business and which were being tracked most rigorously? Which metrics would the direct reports improve as a result of their leaders attending the training? After partnering with some of the businesses and talking to some of their front-line directors, managers, and team leaders, we captured the metrics that were most important to their bottom line. The productivity metrics reported were primarily sales (new customers or merchants acquired) and customer satisfaction. These became our targets and defined how we would quantify "productivity" in our future assessments and analysis. We wanted to make sure we understood the relationship between these specific metrics and the money value or "benefit" we could turn them into.

For Level 3, the first thing we did was interview some key leaders to find out what distinguished the highest performing front-line managers from the worst. What are the things they do every day to drive these higher metrics in their direct reports? The second thing we did for our Level 3 was compare these reported leader behaviors to the ones that were already in the organization-wide leadership competency model. After cross-referencing and comparing these 60+ behaviors, we pared the list down to about 20 that were both readily observable/measurable and crucial to the business. The third thing we did for our Level 3 was compare this list to the list of learning objectives (Level 2) and behaviors that were being pinpointed and targeted by our specific training program. This brought our list of Level 3 leadership behaviors down to a powerful eight. These were the eight behaviors we would include in our Level 3 assessment. Here, we were looking for levels of improvement in these specific behaviors as a result of the training.

Gathering the Data

Participants attending the two-day instructor-led program were given a five-minute survey immediately after training. This survey captured the participants' satisfaction with the experience (*Level 1*) and the level of new knowledge and skills acquired (*Level 2*). Three months after the training was completed, participants were then emailed a link to take another survey online and were instructed to invite their direct reports to complete a similar survey. For participants, this 15-minute survey captured behavior change (*Level 3*) and performance improvements. For direct reports, the survey included questions about their leaders' behavior change (same core questions) and also about how their own performance and productivity improved (*Level 4*). Using these performance increases, a return on investment (ROI) analysis (*Level 5*) was then conducted for all respondents reporting "sales" as their primary performance measure. Also included in participants' self-assessment was a transfer climate index that asked participants about the work environment they returned to post-training (*Level 6*).

What should immediately strike you about the aforementioned approach to data gathering is how simple yet comprehensive it is. We literally collected all the data we needed to develop a complete story of impact (Level 1–6) in less than 20 minutes' worth of assessment questions. This was one of the key selling points to the business leaders and stakeholders. While they initially expressed (as most businesses do) their apprehensiveness and aversion to surveys, they gave us complete buy-in based in part on the speed and simplicity of this approach. We literally told them in so many words, "You spent thousands of dollars on training and pulled so many people away from their jobs for two whole days and now you don't want to take another 20 minutes to find out if it was all worth it?" Not only that, but we then told them through this analysis we'd be able to identify the climate factors that were either helping or hindering their training successes. Presenting them with robust data and creating this new level of evaluation for them was the other key part to securing their sponsorship and continued support throughout the study. This immediately put the added measurement request in perspective and they quickly realized there would be great returns on this relatively small investment.

Results

Level 1 and Level 2

As far as how well the program was received (Level 1) and the amount of learning that took place (Level 2), participants took no more than five minutes to answer a few key questions about their experience. The results of the quantitative questions are shown in figures CS1.2 and CS1.3.

These results show that overall the participants were very happy with the program and did in fact learn leadership skills that were relevant and important to their roles. Though not included in this summary, we did also collect, analyze, and report open-ended comments and themes to support these quantitative results. While these Level 1 and Level 2 results can rarely be used to predict the ultimate

172 • Measuring and Maximizing Training Impact

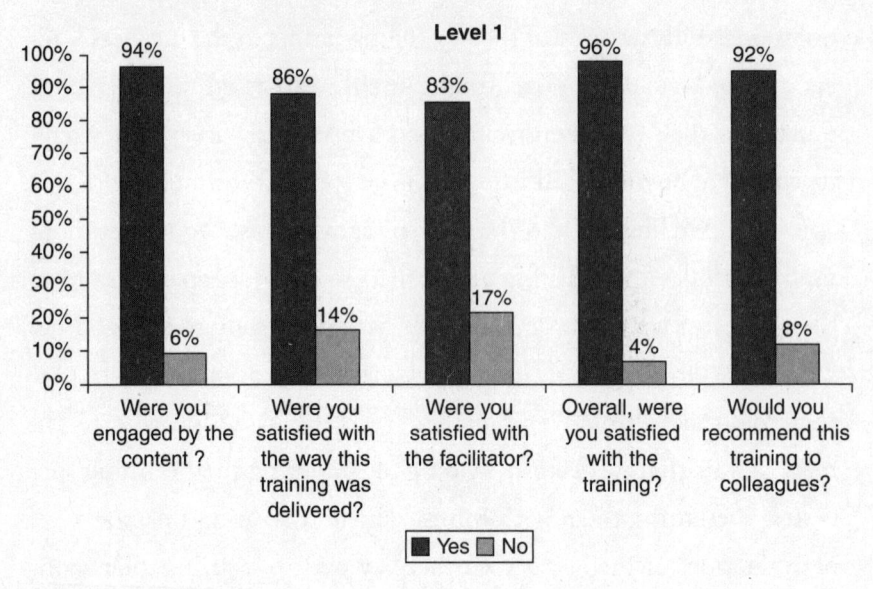

Level 1

Question	Yes	No
Were you engaged by the content?	94%	6%
Were you satisfied with the way this training was delivered?	86%	14%
Were you satisfied with the facilitator?	83%	17%
Overall, were you satisfied with the training?	96%	4%
Would you recommend this training to colleagues?	92%	8%

Figure CS1.2 Level 1 results.

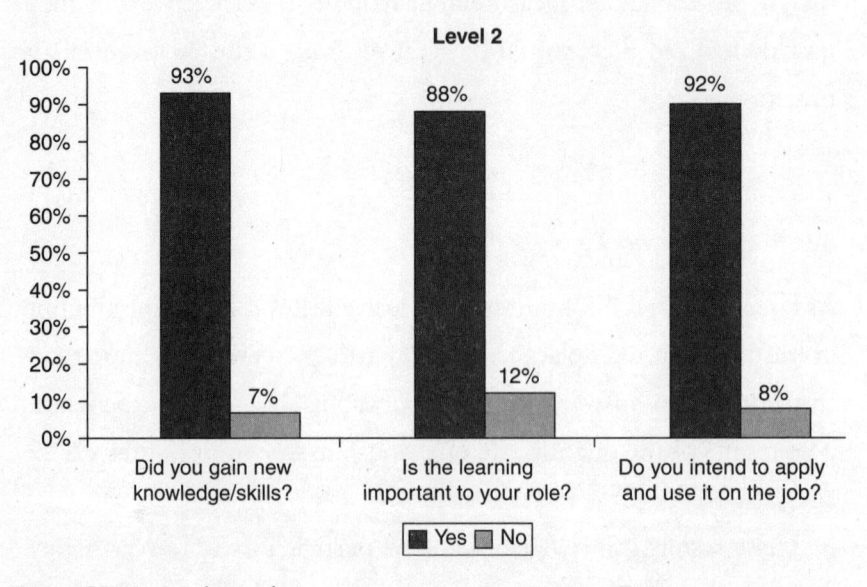

Level 2

Question	Yes	No
Did you gain new knowledge/skills?	93%	7%
Is the learning important to your role?	88%	12%
Do you intend to apply and use it on the job?	92%	8%

Figure CS1.3 Level 2 results.

outcome and ROI of a training program, they are useful to get some preliminary data on how a program is being received. They also provide some important feedback on how to improve the delivery of content and which components provided the best learning.

Level 3

When it came to behavior change (Level 3), we looked at the percentage of participants who were demonstrating observed levels of improvement. Using a six-point improvement scale, we asked both participants and their direct reports to rate the level of improvement they observed in eight critical, training-related behaviors (this number can vary and was primarily defined by what was most observable and critical to the business). One important thing to look for in these results is similarity in the response distributions. That is, did direct reports corroborate the self-ratings? Also note that "high improvement" was defined as the self and direct reports rating a participant's improvement either "significant" or "exceptional" on our scale. As you'll see shortly, we used this valuable group to compare and calculate higher levels of impact. Figure CS1.4 shows our overall response distributions.

Beyond the quantitative results, we also collected qualitative feedback to bring the numbers to life and understand what types of behaviors were most affected and impacted by the training. Here, we asked participants to give examples of the types of improvements they made. After collecting and reading through close to 700 comments (obviously not everyone gave feedback), the responses were bunched by theme and the top three themes or success stories were reported. The top themes, the approximate percentage of comments that fell into each of these themes, and an exemplary quote for each is given in figure CS1.5.

Level 4

Of course the next question was "so what...?" What did high improvements in certain key leader behaviors actually mean to the business? More specifically, how did participants improving their

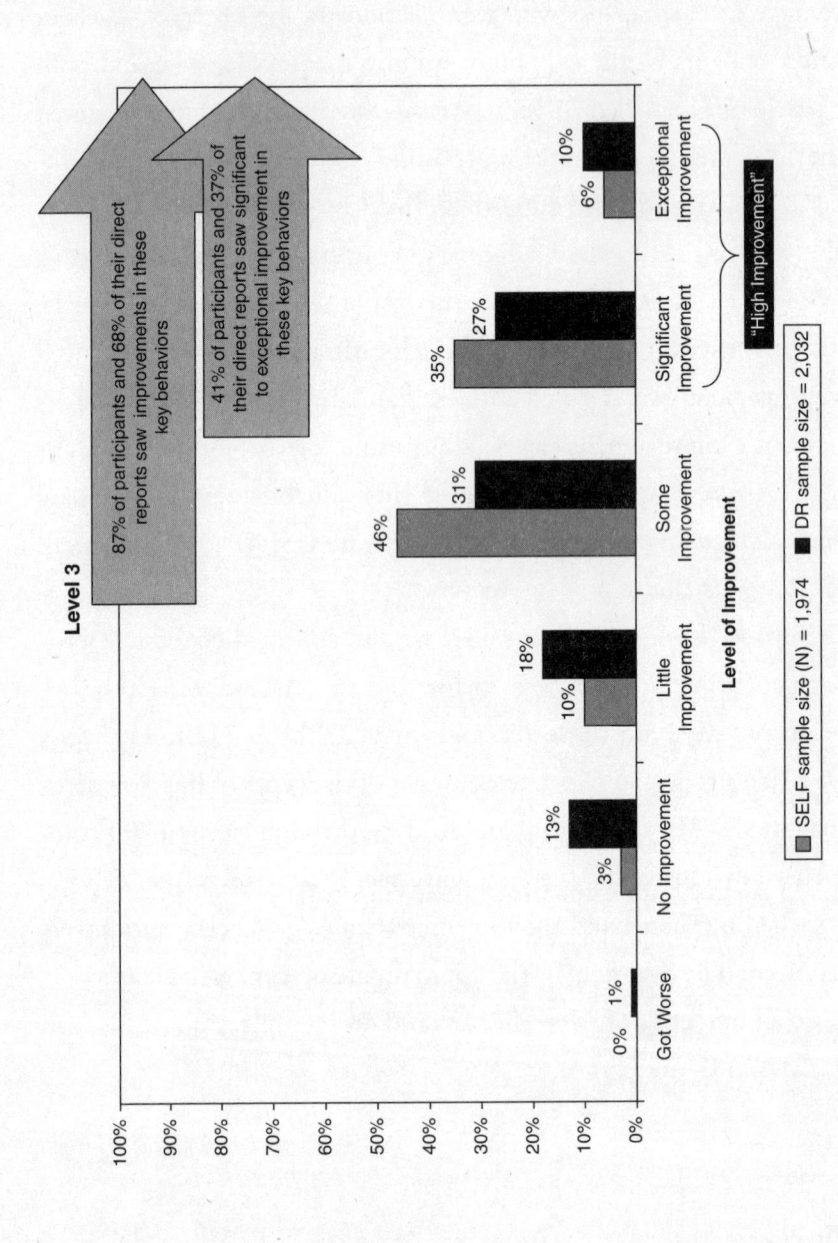

Figure CS1.4 Level 3 results.

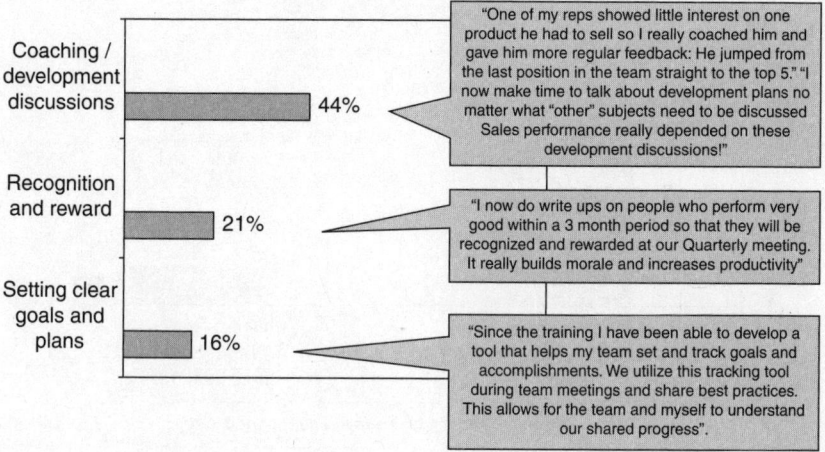

Level 3
"Give a specific example of how you improved leadership performance."
Top 3 Themes (from 746 comments)

Coaching / development discussions — 44%

"One of my reps showed little interest on one product he had to sell so I really coached him and gave him more regular feedback: He jumped from the last position in the team straight to the top 5." "I now make time to talk about development plans no matter what "other" subjects need to be discussed Sales performance really depended on these development discussions!"

Recognition and reward — 21%

"I now do write ups on people who perform very good within a 3 month period so that they will be recognized and rewarded at our Quarterly meeting. It really builds morale and increases productivity"

Setting clear goals and plans — 16%

"Since the training I have been able to develop a tool that helps my team set and track goals and accomplishments. We utilize this tracking tool during team meetings and share best practices. This allows for the team and myself to understand our shared progress".

Figure CS1.5 Qualitative results for Level 3.

leadership behaviors actually affect their direct reports' levels of productivity? This brought us to our Level 4 measure—Business Impact.

The first step in proving business impact was showing a strong relationship between behavior improvements and productivity gains. That is, did leaders who made great improvements in their leadership competencies (Level 3 scores) have direct reports who also made greater improvements in their performance and productivity? Conversely, did leaders who improved nothing back on the job (or nearly nothing) have direct reports who showed reflectively lower levels of productivity gains?

Here we separated our entire sample of direct reports into two distinct groups: Group A, direct reports of "high improvement" leaders, versus Group B, direct reports of "no improvement" leaders. When we looked at the extent to which each of these two groups of direct reports improved their primary measures of performance (in this case sales), some significant and impressive differences emerged.

Level 4
PRODUCTIVITY INCREASES OF DIRECT REPORTS

[Bar chart showing:
- Direct Reports of "High Improvement" Leaders: 44%
- Direct Reports of "No Improvement" Leaders: 11%
- Legend: = Productivity Gains (average reported in %)]

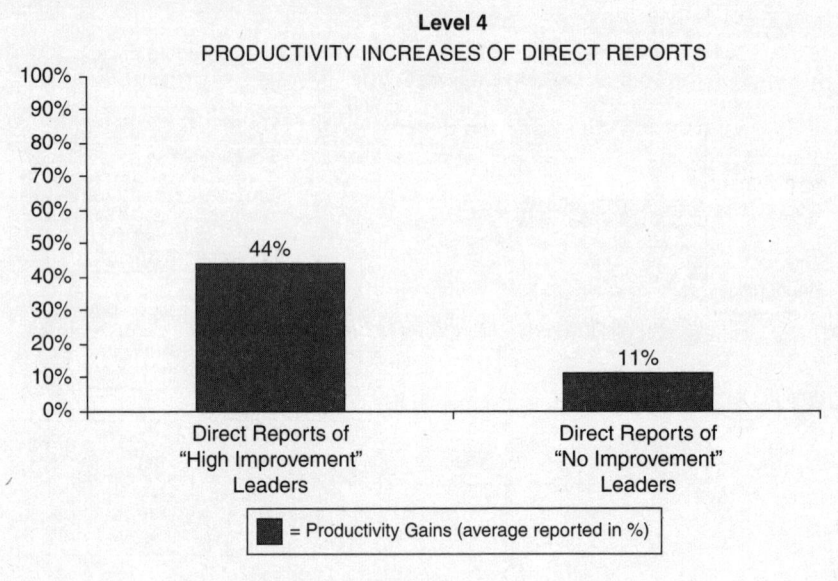

Figure CS1.6 Level 4 productivity differences.

The direct reports of "high improvement" leaders were increasing their productivity by an average of 44 percent over the recent three months since training, while the direct reports of "no improvement" leaders showed increases of only 11 percent over that same period (see figure CS1.6).

The great thing about this comparison and the reason why it was presented here was because it effectively controls for all other factors that could be affecting increases in sales and simply compares the two groups based on leadership differences. This comparison can easily be made without worrying about all the other internal and external factors that can influence productivity because each group here is influenced equally by those extraneous factors. For instance, the first question the business had was—How can you isolate the effect of this training when so many things were changing in the market over those three months? My simple answer to that was—"It doesn't matter how much the market changed, declined, or improved because both these groups had employees who sold during the same exact period under the same exact market conditions." In fact, even direct reports of "No improvement leaders" were showing increases of 11 percent so obviously there were other factors making people increase their metrics (e.g., new market segments, new products or services available, etc.). The point is that it doesn't matter what's happening out there because our only concern is comparing the raw differences between these two groups. This principle holds true for any other demographic that might have confounded our measures. As long as we had equally represented regions, tenures, type of products sold, and so on in both groups, we could perform our Level 4 analyses without fear of the typical factors that could confound our study.

Another question that came from the business was—How can you rely on the estimates of employees when it comes to productivity improvements? Working on the same principle, the simple answer to that question was—"The inaccuracy or tendency to overrate productivity also doesn't matter here because it shows up equally for all employees in both groups." That is, while some individuals may be prone to overestimating productivity, that bias error will be present for employees in both groups. Another aspect of this study that assuaged this bias concern was the size of the samples. The more people you have, the lower the error of the estimate. As with the first question from our business partners, the power of this Level 4 design comes from comparing simple increases in productivity between the groups. In this case, the impressive difference was a 44 percent increase in sales for employees who had highly improved leaders, compared to only an 11 percent for those reporting to non-improvement leaders.

While this makes an incredible case for how the behavior of a leader can impact productivity and clearly shows that there is a significant "effect," this analysis does not reflect the true impact experienced across the organization. That is, we compared two polar data sets to determine if there was an effect created by the independent variable (leadership), but now we have to define and isolate the impact of that effect across the organization. After all, we clearly knew from the data that not all participants were impacted equally by the training. Some participants were affected less, while some were not affected at all by the training. The overall impact of the training will be determined by taking the magnitude or depth of the effect and combining that with the scope or breadth of the effect—the amount of people that were actually affected. It is the function of these two numbers that will determine your training's "overall effect size."

Calculating a Leadership "Effect Size"

To isolate and calculate our overall effect size, we needed to determine two things: first, the size of the effect, which tells us the strength of the training when applied correctly; and second, the size of the effected population, which tells us the breadth and scope of this effect across the organization. We determined the amount of the "effect" by simply calculating the productivity difference between the two groups: 44 percent − 11 percent = *33 percent*. Then, to calculate the "effected" population, we simply looked at how many direct reports from the entire population (N = 2,032) ended up with "High Improvement Leaders." Note, the "Little Improvement" and especially the "Some Improvement" leaders could have been bunched into this calculation as part of the "effected" population, but in an effort to remain ultraconservative with our calculations and estimates of impact, we chose not to include them. Here, we found that *37 percent* of all the direct reports had "high improvement leaders" and that gave me a "total effect size" of *12 percent (33 percent X 37 percent = 12 percent)* (see figure CS1.7).

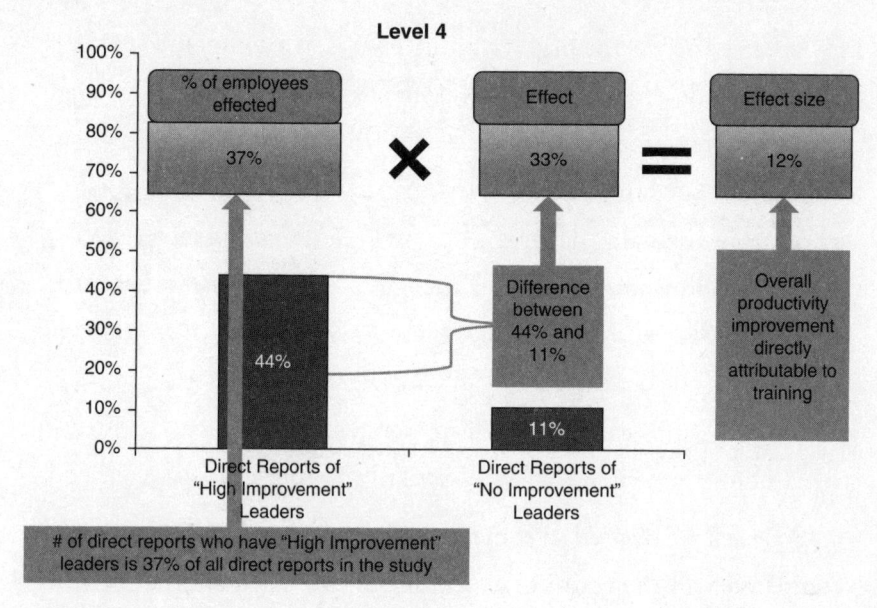

Figure CS1.7 Calculating an overall effect size.

From these results we saw that direct reports increased their sales productivity by an overall average of 12 percent as a direct outcome of their leaders attending the leadership training. These Level 4 results were significant and demonstrated training had a powerful impact across the organization. Remember, some employees might have seen tremendous impact and some far less, but accounting for these two scenarios, and everyone in between, is the *average* overall impact per participant. Turning all these aggregate numbers into the *average productivity increase per participant* makes it easier to progress our evaluation story and talk about the overall effect size of our training. This also makes it easier to compare it to the average cost per participant in our Level 5.

Level 5—ROI

Our next step was to monetize these organizational benefits and determine the extent of this impact on the bottom line. What does

180 • Measuring and Maximizing Training Impact

Level 5
ROI
What does a 12% increase in productivity mean in $ benefit?

Over a 3 month period a sales specialist contributes an average of $50,000 in revenue. A 12% increase above $50,000 would be $6,000

- 12% increase in sales revenue $6,000..Benefit = $6,000
- Amount of employees (per participant) increasing sales..5
- Total benefit per participant..Total Benefit = $30,000

- The investment per participant..Cost = $2,000

- The Return on Investment* ....ROI = 1400%

$$**ROI\% = \frac{Benefit - Cost}{Cost} \times 100$$

Figure CS1.8 Calculating the ROI for leadership training.

a *12 percent increase in sales* mean in dollar value and how does that compare to all the training expenditures? To calculate the ROI, we looked at all employees reporting sales revenue as their primary productivity metric. According to the business, the average sales specialist from this target group contributed approximately $50,000 in revenue (calculated in part by the benefit and projection of spending by new customers acquired) over a three-month period. If this employee's contribution was to increase by 12 percent due to better direction and support from his/her leader, the added benefit to the company would be approximately $6,000. Now consider that each leader in the study impacted not one employee, but had an average of five employees that were being directly influenced every day by his/her behaviors. That brings the total benefit for the company to *$30,000* (6000 X 5). If the benefit is $30,000 in additional revenue, and the cost of the training was approximately $2,000, the return on investment is *1,400 percent* (see formula and calculation in figure CS1.8).

Level 6—Transfer Climate

Which factors in the participant's immediate work environment were predictive of how much training would be applied and sustained on the job? To measure these crucial make or break factors and identify the *top three* we used the results of our "transfer climate index." These items were attached to the three-month postprogram survey that included all our Level 3 and Level 4 questions. Here, we essentially correlated the scores on the transfer climate questions to the scores on the questions about behavior change and performance improvements. When we looked at the results of this analysis, we found three environmental or climate factors that were consistently predicting whether a learner would have "no improvement" or "high improvement" back on the job. These factors were:

- Their manager follows up with them and has one-on-one meetings after the event to discuss what was learned and how to apply.
- Their manager endorses the training and supports their development.
- Their manager specifically recognizes and rewards the improved leadership behaviors.

Figure CS1.9 depicts just how much these factors could discriminate between levels of impact. For example, if you look at the first set of data on the left, 74 percent of learners in the "high improvement" group were having one-on-one conversations about how to apply their training, while only 13 percent of the "no improvement" group were having these same conversations. In fact, all three factors were present and pervasive for the "high improvement" group, while they were all significantly lower for the "no improvement" group.

Conclusion

When it comes to ROI, the training that can (and should) pack the biggest punch is your leadership training. When leaders increase

Level 6

how DO climate factors affect improvement and impact?

Critical Incidence Analysis:

- Has conversations with leader about how to apply training: No Improvement Group 16%, High Improvement Group 85%
- Has a leader who endorses training: No Improvement Group 25%, High Improvement Group 80%
- Expects to be rewarded for improved behaviors: No Improvement Group 30%, High Improvement Group 79%

79% of employees in the high improvement group expect to be rewarded when they apply the training

30% of employees in the no improvement group expect to be rewarded when they apply the training

Transfer Climate Factors

■ No Improvement Group ■ High Improvement Group

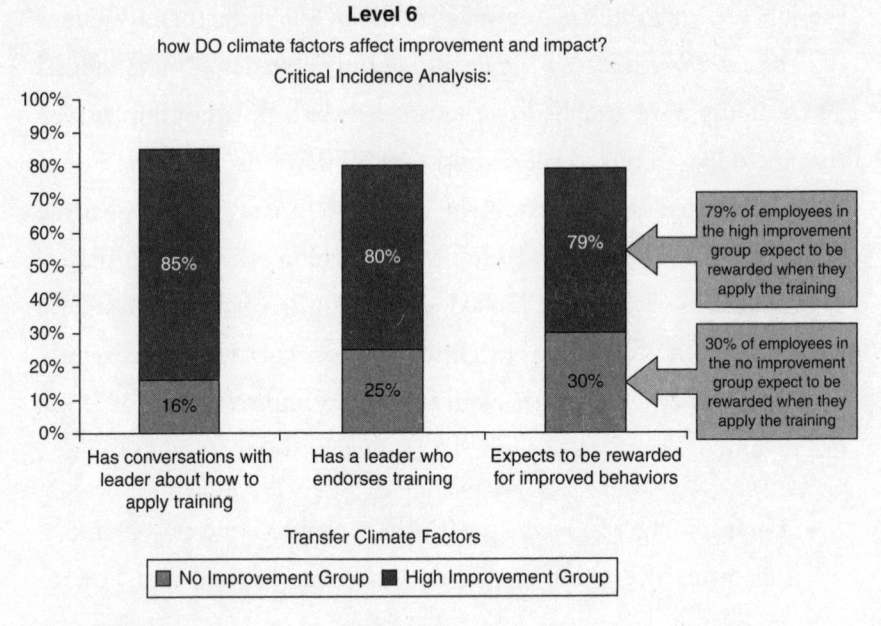

Figure CS1.9 Level 6—critical climate factors.

their effort and improve their leadership behaviors on the job, they not only become more productive, but they have a tremendous, positive ripple effect on all the employees they lead and influence every day. If captured and measured correctly, the "benefit" of these leader improvements can result in some stunning returns. I call this the *"Leadership ROI."*

For this particular study, it was shown that a significant number of leaders improved their leadership behaviors and were doing a few crucial things different after the training. These changes by the leaders clearly made their immediate direct reports more productive on the job. In fact, these direct reports, on average, showed a 12 percent increase in productivity (measured by sales revenues) in the three months after their leader attended the training. Each leader also had an average of five immediate direct reports who were being influenced every day by his or her leadership. That meant for every *one* leader that attended the training and did a few things different afterwards, there were *five* employees that were enhancing their performance and improving their primary business metric, which in this case was sales. This led to a final ROI for each training participant of 1,400 percent. This is the power of the leadership ROI.

What our evaluation also told us was that participants were clearly taking their learning back to very different work environments, and these often disparate "climates" had a profound effect on how well they applied the training. That is, those who had tactical support from their immediate leader and were deliberately rewarded for their training-related changes were demonstrating far greater improvement and impact than those who had less supportive environments. Further, the results of this Level 6 analysis told us which specific climate factors were having the biggest quantifiable influence on the training outcomes and ROI. Imagine the power of knowing what your top factors are and very precisely targeting them for future training rollouts and initiatives. Considering how much they could improve their training's impact and ROI by making their participants' climate more conducive to learning transfer, the simple decision to measure and evaluate was one that had immediate payoffs. The fact that the same training can result in either a 0 percent ROI or a 1,400 percent ROI depending on these climate factors truly demonstrated the power and urgency to measure the impact of training all the way through level 6.

From these results, it should also be clear that measuring and reporting the impact of your leadership training is not only achievable, but also quite simple if you create the right strategy and design. In total, the time I asked from participants for this entire evaluation was no more than 20–25 minutes. While I spent some more time behind the scenes getting to understand the behaviors and business metrics we needed to include, it all still added up to a small drop in the bucket compared to the time and resources an organization spends launching any one given training program. By investing just a little in your measurement strategy, and asking a few simple questions, to the right employees, at the right times, you can end up a few months later telling an incredible story of bottom-line impact. How's that for an ROI?

CASE STUDY 2

Maximizing the Impact of Leadership Training through Different Delivery Modes

Once we had a solid Level 1–6 measurement strategy in place and we knew we could accurately measure the impact and ROI of this particular training program, we were then in a perfect position to measure some different delivery modes to determine which one would yield the highest returns. Here, the primary objective was to maximize our ROI by analyzing and comparing the effectiveness of three primary delivery modes: online versus instructor-led versus a blended approach. While companies all over the world are making crucial decisions and spending billions of dollars on these various delivery modes, there exists little to no quantitative research to support their ultimate decisions. That is, which delivery mode is truly more effective and which will give you the greatest return on your training dollars?

Comparing Online versus Classroom versus Blended Delivery

The crucial first step of this study was to define or operationalize what we really meant by each mode of delivery. The "online" group was defined as those employees who experienced all aspects of the training online. They accessed everything they needed through a learning management system and then proceeded through a completely self-directed experience. They had absolutely no formal supporting events or instruction to supplement the training. The "instructor-led" group was defined as those who attended a one-day, facilitator-run classroom event. This was an abridged version of the two-day training described in the previous study. There was no formal prework or postwork to support the event. Here, instructors were either provided externally by the vendor or trained internally to deliver the course content. The "blended" group was defined as those employees who experienced a hybrid approach consisting of a classroom-type kick-off event (virtual for most employees) led by a popular business leader, a self-directed online portion that was completed on their own time, and a classroom wrap-up (also virtual for most employees) that was held six weeks after the completion of training. The kick-off event brought employees together to set and discuss expectations, the web-based learning lasted for approximately six hours and presented concepts scenarios and exercises, and the wrap-up encouraged all participants to talk about what they learned with their peers and managers. Here, they discussed their biggest lessons learned and how best to apply their training back on the job with their direct reports.

Training delivery options: People leaders were offered three different delivery modes. The sample sizes for each group are indicated here:

- *Online*: completely self-directed online experience; N = 203
- *Instructor-led*: classroom setting with facilitator; N = 394
- *Blended*: combination of online learning and instructor-led kick-off and wrap-up; N = 402

Table CS2.1 Level 1–6 evaluation approach

Measurement	Method of evaluation
Level 1: Reaction	Learner responds to survey upon completion of learning event (satisfaction with experience)
Level 2: Knowledge	Learner responds to survey upon completion of learning event (new knowledge and skills acquired)
Level 3: Behavior	Assessment completed by manager, self, and direct reports three months after learning event (observed improvement in leadership skills)
Level 4: Impact	Assessment completed by manager, self, and direct reports three months after learning event (improved productivity of direct reports)
Level 5: ROI	Cost vs. benefit analysis based on increase in sales productivity of direct reports over three months
Level 6: Transfer Climate	Assesses factors in participant's work environment (climate) that will help or hinder the transfer of learning

Evaluation Approach

For this study, the evaluation and overall impact of each of the training delivery modes was measured using the same traditional five-level approach and again included a Level 6 analysis to identify the strongest predictors of business impact. While most of the methodology for collecting data was the same as the previous case study, this one actually added the direct leaders of the participants as one more data point to corroborate behavior change and performance improvements. See summary of Level 1–6 measurement approach in table CS2.1.

Gathering the Data

Participants were given a survey immediately after attending the leadership program. This survey captured satisfaction with the experience and the level of new knowledge and skills acquired (Levels 1 and 2). Three months after the training was completed, participants were then emailed a link to take another survey online. Within this same email they were instructed to invite both their leaders and their direct reports to complete a similar online survey. All three surveys included the same core questions capturing behavior change and application (Level 3), as well as increases in productivity and performance (Level 4). A return on investment analysis (Level 5) was then conducted for all participants reporting a "sales revenue" metric as their primary measure of performance. Included in the self-assessment for the actual training participants was a transfer climate index that asked participants about the work environment and climates they returned to post-training (Level 6). The quantitative results at each of the six levels were carefully analyzed and compared.

Results

Level 1 and Level 2

When we measured the reaction to the program (Level 1) and the amount of learning that took place (Level 2), all three modes of delivery received similar high ratings. Here, to make it easier to compare results across delivery modes, we included rating scales (possible 1–5) instead of the typical Yes/No options for two core questions:

Level 1: Overall, were you satisfied with the training?
Level 2: Did you gain valuable new knowledge and skills from this training?

As you can see from figure CS2.1, there was not much variability in the responses and all ratings were between 4.25 and 4.55 for both Level 1 and Level 2 questions. Although the instructor-led training seemed to inch out the other two modes at both Levels 1 and 2, the differences were not significant enough to draw any conclusions about the delivery mode. As I mentioned in the previous case study, these often skewed results at the Level 1 and Level 2 stages make it

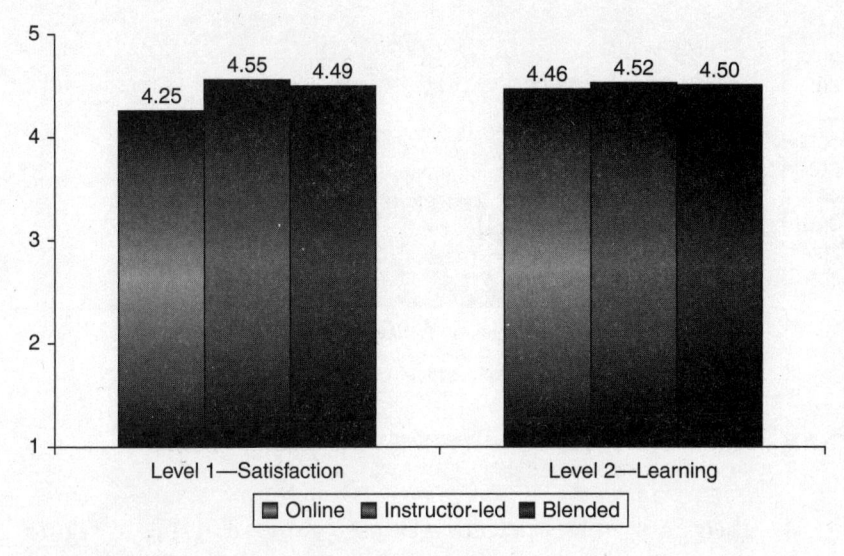

Figure CS2.1 Comparison of Level 1 and 2 scores.

hard to form solid correlations and predictions about higher levels of evaluation and impact. That being said, if there were any delivery modes that were significantly inferior or profoundly ineffective for participants, the results at these levels would have demonstrated and told us that.

Level 3

In order to measure and compare application and improvement in the key leadership behaviors (Level 3) across delivery modes, we first looked at the percentage of participants who were demonstrating "high improvement" in each of groups. That is, how many employees (what percentage of the population) in the online group were rated as high improvement, how many in the instructor-led group were rated as high improvement, and how many in the blended group? Remember, this category of high improvement meant the ratings of these participants were either "significant" or "exceptional" on our scale.

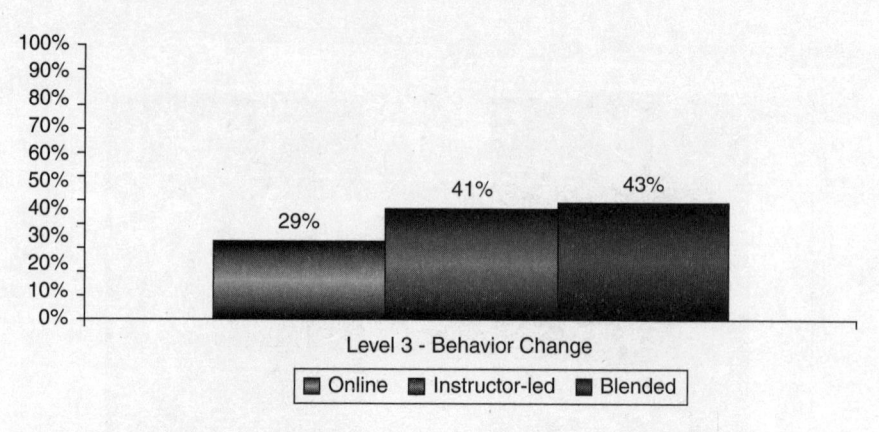

Figure CS2.2 Comparison of Level 3 improvement.

We then took these percentages and compared them. Figure CS2.2 shows the comparisons. For the self-directed web-based program there were 29 percent of participants showing high improvement, for the instructor-led program there were 41 percent showing high improvement, and for the blended approach it was 43 percent. These findings clearly indicate distinct and significant differences in training impact, with the instructor-led approach being more effective than the online approach and the blended approach proving to be more effective than both of the other delivery modes.

Level 4

For our Level 4 analyses and comparison, we calculated an "overall effect size" for each of the different delivery modes. The "overall effect size" is the amount of overall productivity increase (of the direct reports) that can be directly attributed to the training. To get this number for each delivery mode we first calculated the "effect" of applying the training, and then multiplied that number by the amount of "effected" employees. For instance, for the online training, we separated the sample of direct reports into two distinct groups: Group A, direct reports of "high improvement" leaders (high Level 3 scores), versus Group B, direct reports of "no improvement" leaders (low Level 3 scores). We then compared the productivity improvements for each of these groups (30 percent for the direct reports of high improvement leaders vs. 13 percent for the direct reports of low improvement leaders). The raw difference between these numbers became the "effect" the training had on productivity if it was applied correctly and the leaders improved their leadership performance (30 percent – 13 percent = 17 percent). Since not everyone applied the training, improved their skills, and impacted their direct reports productivity, we then had to adjust this number by taking into account only those employees that were significantly affected by the training—employees that were originally in the high improvement group (29 percent). When we multiplied the effect (17 percent) by the amount of those affected (29 percent), we ended up with the overall effect size of the online training program equaling 5 percent. The effect size and the Level 4 calculation are depicted in figure CS2.3.

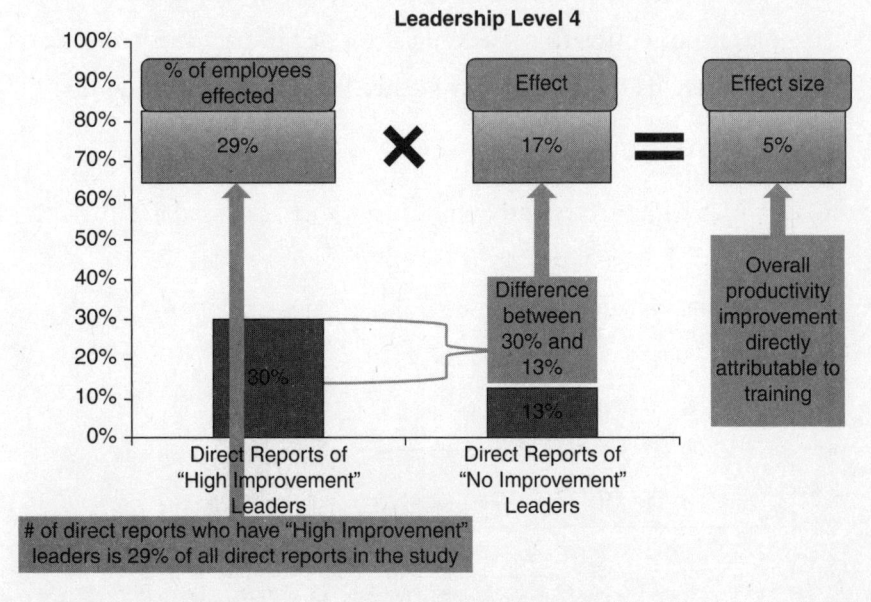

Figure CS2.3 Calculating a Level 4 "effect size" for online training.

192 • Measuring and Maximizing Training Impact

When we did this same analysis for the instructor-led delivery we ended up with an overall effect size of 11 percent. The same analysis for the blended approach yielded an overall effect size of 13 percent. The data used to calculate the overall effect size for each of the delivery modes are provided in figure CS2.4, which compares the Level 4 results for each of the different delivery modes.

Delivery mode	Effect (%)	Employees effected (%)	Overall effect size (%)
Instructor-led	28	41	11
Online	17	29	5
Blended	31	43	13

The great thing about this data was it told a consistent story from Level 3 to Level 4. That is, the training group that was seeing the most behavioral improvements from their participants (blended group) was also the one seeing the highest increase in sales productivity (percentage increase in sales revenue). Similarly, the training group that was seeing the lowest improvements from their participants was also the one with the lowest increase in sales productivity. This pattern or correlation was crucial for our impact story to make sense and gave us the consistency we needed to confidently compare

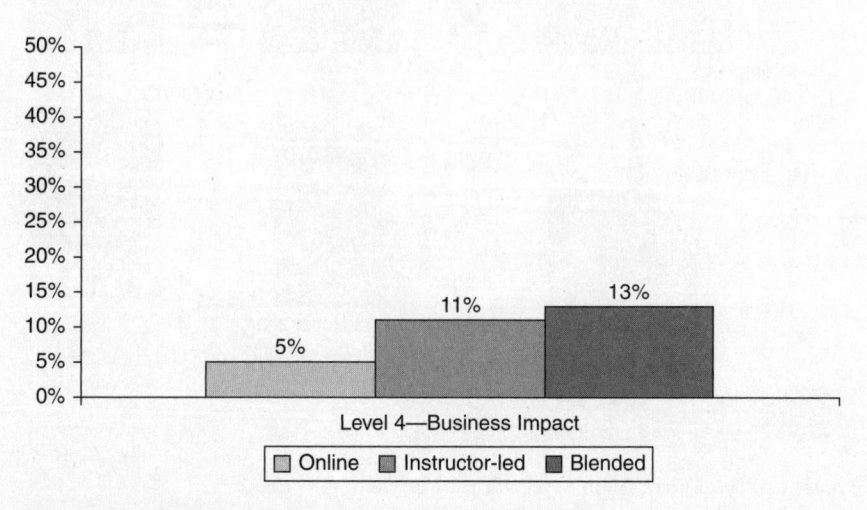

Figure CS2.4 Overall effect sizes compared across delivery modes.

across delivery modes. These robust findings gave us solid ground and sure footing to step into our Level 5 ROI comparison.

Level 5—ROI

For our Level 5 analysis we turned each of these productivity increases into real dollar "benefits" for the business. That is, we asked what does a 5-, 11-, or 13-percent increase in sales ultimately mean to the bottom line? To do this we took the average sales revenue generated per three months per sales specialist (three months because that was the duration of the post-training period) and then simply multiplied that by each of the increases. For example, the average sales specialist from this sample generated $55,000 in revenue over a three-month period. This meant for the online training, where employees increased sales by 5 percent due to better direction and support from their leaders, the ultimate benefit to the business was $2,750 (55,000 × .05). For the instructor-led training, where the employees increased sales by 11 percent, it meant $6,050 to the business; and for the blended approach, where there was a 13-percent increase in sales, it meant $7,150 to the business.

Now consider that each leader (participant) in this study impacted not one direct sales employee, but, on average, five employees. That is, each of these trainees had an average of five direct reports that were being influenced every day by their leadership improvements and increasing their productivity. This meant we had to take each of the monetary benefits realized by each delivery mode and multiply it by five. See the average impact per leader, per delivery mode in table CS2.2.

Table CS2.2 Training benefits across delivery modes

Delivery mode	Sales improvement per employee (in $)	Number of employees per participant	Overall sales improvement per participant (in $)
Instructor-led	6,050	5	30,250
Online	2,750	5	13,750
Blended	7,150	5	35,750

Once we had the "benefits" of our leadership training for each delivery mode, we then just needed to compare them to the cost of each approach. This meant itemizing and collecting information on all the implementation costs (development, materials, staffing, etc.) as well as the invitation costs (registration fees, travel, time away from jobs, etc.). To calculate our ROI we used the classic formula:

$$\text{ROI\%} = \frac{\text{Benefit} - \text{Cost}}{\text{Cost}} \times 100$$

This final ROI analysis allowed us to compare the true ROI of each delivery mode and determine which had the greatest impact on the bottom line. The data and results are presented in table CS2.3.

The results of this ROI analysis told a critical story about the ultimate payoff of each delivery mode. There were three glaring conclusions from the data:

1. Although the "benefits" of the instructor-led training were more than double that of the online training, the ROIs for each of these were not much different because the cost of the online delivery was almost half the cost of the instructor-led delivery mode.
2. While the benefits of the blended approach and the instructor-led approach were similar, the blended delivery mode realized an ROI that was approximately 75 percent greater than the instructor-led because it was significantly cheaper to deliver.
3. Overall the blended approach outperformed both the web-based and the instructor-led approach by yielding higher benefits while simultaneously keeping costs down. This resulted in an ROI about 75 percent higher than the instructor-led and more than double that of the online delivery mode.

Table CS2.3 Benefits, costs, and final ROI results for each delivery mode

	Instructor-led training	*Online learning*	*Blended learning*
Total benefit per leader	$30,250	$13,750	$35,750
Total cost per leader	$2,300	$1,300	$1,600
Return on investment	1,215%	958%	2,134%

Level 6—Transfer Climate

So What Was It about the "Blended" Approach That Made It More Effective?

The simple answer to this question is—Transfer Climate. The transfer climate describes the factors in the participant's immediate work environment that predict how much training will be applied and sustained on the job. To measure these factors and identify those that are most important to transfer, we attached a "transfer climate assessment" to the Level 3 and Level 4 postprogram impact survey. When we looked at the work environments that these learners were going back to post-training, we found some specific factors that were consistently predicting whether a learner would have "no improvement" or "high improvement." Like the previous study, these factors were:

1. Did the learner have one-on-one meetings with his/her immediate manager after the training to discuss how to apply the training in his/her specific role?
2. Did the learner perceive his/her manager endorsed and supported this specific training?
3. Did the learner expect to be recognized or rewarded for the training-related behavior change?

If this analysis was correct, and these were the factors that were predicting the greatest impact, then the delivery mode that fostered these climate elements the most would be the most effective and deliver the greatest ROI. This is exactly what happened in this study.

Learners that took the blended approach had the highest scores on all three of these post-training factors and consequently had the best results. These participants were having significant and sustained impact from their training and were clearly taking their learning back to a different work environment. Also notice that these three factors are all very directly influenced by the participants' immediate managers. This proved one of our major hypotheses—an immediate leader has the potential to either make or break any training effort.

So to answer our original Level 6 question: the real reason why the blended solution was more effective was because it fostered an environment of manager involvement and accountability. With intentional components like leader-led "kick-offs" and "wrap-ups," and follow-up conversations with immediate managers built right into to the blended approach, it's not surprising that this group of learners were more effectively "transferring" the learning back to their jobs. In fact, the climate was so important to the impact of the training that when the climate was held constant across all delivery modes (where online, instructor-led, and blended training participants had equally supportive climates) there ended up being no significant differences in impact. Here, we found that the climate was really predicting the impact and not necessarily the delivery mode. In other words, if you build a great transfer climate, any training delivery mode can be equally effective and the ROI will truly be maximized. The blended approach had more positive results simply because it had the right climate factors built right into the training design. This led to the high climate, which led to higher improvement in leader competencies, which led to greater impact on the business, and finally greater ROI.

Conclusion

In this study we compared the impact and ROI of three distinct training delivery options: Online courses with no formal support structure; instructor-led classroom training events with no online or other support structure; and a blended learning solution combining both online and classroom training, including kick-off and wrap-up events, as well as supportive discussions throughout the courses. Based on the traditional five levels of evaluation and some brand new methods for calculating effects at each level, we found that the blended learning approach, which created and fostered a climate of high immediate manager support, offered higher impact and a significantly greater ROI than the other two delivery modes. However, through deeper analysis, we found that each delivery mode could feasibly offer the same impact as long as the climate elements (especially the leader support) were held constant.

While the traditional levels of evaluation told us a critical story about the effectiveness and ROI of each delivery mode the Level 6 Transfer Climate measure told us an even more important story—it told us why we got these results in the first place and how we can improve the impact of each delivery mode in the future. It explained why training was far more effective for some groups over others and also informed the business groups what they can do to maximize the effects of their employees' training as they roll it out in the future.

These findings clearly indicate that the true impact of a training program will best be predicted by the work climate each participant returns to after the event. In this study, the type of leader they work with and report to after their training made the biggest difference. With leaders at all levels of an organization being able to make or break the effects of these training programs, the importance of understanding and creating a high transfer climate should be paramount for any training initiatives or strategies. As clearly evidenced in this research, the right leader with the right approach will truly work wonders to maximize your training investments.

Index

accountability
  blended solution and, 196
  Level 4 and, 93, 95–6
  Level 6 and, 121–2, 196
  performance metrics and, 82
  shifting for sucess, 95–6
Analysis of Variance (ANOVA), 88
anecdotes, 6, 69, 162

behavior change and application, 12
  see also Level 3
behavioral indicators, 57–60, 134, 166
benefits
  calculating, 104–8, 110
  competency models and, 61
  direct, 104–5
  identifying, 13, 162
  indirect, 105–7
  leader endorsement and, 145
  Level 6 and, 121–3
  measuring, 76, 169
  ROI and, 13–14, 96, 101, 111–14, 153, 179–80, 182, 187, 193–4
bias, 39–40, 43, 46, 86, 90–1, 177
blended learning approach, 149, 185–6, 189–90, 192–7
bridge
  building, 6–10
  building support pillars, 8–10
  creating clear path, 6–8
  evaluating levels, 10–16
  evaluation level 6, 4–6
  overview, 1–2
  path, 2–3
  pillars, 3–4

business impact, 12–13
  see also Level 4
business metrics
  defined, 75–6
  participants' impact on, 76–7

call to action, 121
case studies
  impact of leadership training
    calculating effect size, 178–9
    company background, 166–7
    conclusion, 181–4
    data gathering, 170–1
    evaluation strategy, 168–9
    Level 1 and 2 results, 171–2
    Level 3 results, 173–5
    Level 4 results, 173, 175–8
    Level 5 results, 179–80
    Level 6 results, 180–1
    overview, 165–6
    results, 171–8
    ROI, 179–80
    training, 167
    transfer climate, 180–1
  maximizing impact of leadership training
    comparing delivery modes, 185–7
    conclusion, 196–7
    data gathering, 187–8
    evaluation approach, 187
    Level 1 and 2 results, 188–9
    Level 3 results, 189–90
    Level 4 results, 190–2
    Level 5 results, 193–5
    Level 6 results, 195–6
    ROI, 193–5
    transfer climate, 195–6

Index

clear path, creating, 6–8
climate assessment
   see Transfer Climate Assessment
climate factors, 118–20
   see also Transfer Climate Assessment
competency models
   behavior indicators, 60–1
   benefits of using, 61–2
   overview, 59–60
compliance, 29
control groups, 79, 90, 146
core questions, 17–21
cost, calculating
   diagram, 110
   implementation, 108
   invitation, 108–11
credibility, 14, 66, 111
customer satisfaction (CUSTSAT), 106
   see also satisfaction, customers and

data (collecting, analyzing, and reporting)
   Level 1, 17–21
   Level 2, 27
   Level 3, 37–8
   Level 4, 73–5
   Level 5, 103–4
   Level 6, 117–21
design, choosing
   choosing behaviors, 47–8
   defining domain of behaviors, 52–5
   identifying biggest business drivers, 58–9
   identifying most observable behaviors, 55–7
   making business case, 48–52
   measurement and, 38–9
   post-tests and, 45–7
   problems with assessments, 42–5
   room for improvement, 39–42
difference scores, 11, 30, 39–42, 46
direct reports
   competency models and, 61
   leadership training and, 76–7, 97–100, 126, 165–70, 178–9, 182
   Level 3 and, 65–8, 70–1, 173
   Level 4 and, 76–7, 97–100, 175–7, 190–1
   ROI and, 113–14, 178–9
   training evaluation and, 32–3, 186–8

effect size, 78, 85, 88–93, 97–9, 159, 178–81, 190–2
   calculating, 89–93, 97–9
   control group and, 90
   defining effected population, 92
   explained, 88–9
   homogeneity and, 90–1
   leadership training and, 97–9
   steps, 89–91
effects, linking to training, 78–80
environment
   bridge and, 2
   climate assessment and, 134, 138, 149
   effect on survey results, 79, 90
   Level 3 surveys and, 47, 63, 67
   Level 6 surveys and, 117–19
   training and, 8, 15, 79, 116, 121–3
error of the estimate, 85, 177

homogeneity, 82, 85–6, 90

implementation cost, 108
improvement scale, 45–7, 64
initiative, training and, 50–1
invitation cost, 108–11

kick-offs, 149, 186, 196–7
Kirkpatrick, Donald, 10, 168
knowledge assessments, 29

leader endorsement, 124, 126–7, 140–2, 144–5, 181, 195
leadership training
   calculating ROI for, 113–15, 158, 179–80
   effect size and, 97–9, 178–9
   evaluation of, 53, 60, 64–72
   evaluation strategy, 168–70
   example, 166–7
   gathering data for, 170–1
   improvement due to, 77
   Levels 1–2 and, 171–2
   Level 3 and, 173
   Level 4 and, 96–7, 173–8
   overview, 165–7, 181–4
   qualitative results of, 67–72
   quantitative results of, 64–7
   transfer climate and, 180–1
learning and skill application, 11–12
   see also Level 2

learning initiative, training and, 50
Level 1
   core questions, 17–21
   example survey, 23
   gathering data and creating reports, 23–5
   how to collect, analyze and report data, 17–21
   overview, 10–11
   qualitative results, 24–5
   quantitative results, 24
   scaling survey questions, 21–3
Level 2
   combining with Level 1, 33–6
   how to collect, analyze, and report data, 27
   knowledge assessments, 29
   overview, 11–12
   post-test approach, 28–32
   pre-test approach, 27–8
   qualitative results for, 33
   quantitative results for, 33
   sample survey, 32
Level 3
   choosing your behaviors, 47–8
   choosing your design, 38–9
   crafting survey, 62–72
   domain of behaviors, 52–3
   focusing your evaluation, 52–9
   how to collect, analyze, and report data, 37–8
   identifying biggest business drivers, 58–9
   identifying most observable behaviors, 55–7
   making your business case, 48–52
   measurement, 38–9
   overview, 12
   picking the right leadership behaviors, 54
   post-test assessments, 45–7
   problems with assessments, 42–5
   qualitative questions, 67–72
   quantitative questions, 62–7
   questions with improvement scale, 64
   reporting results, 64–7, 70–2
   response distribution, 65
   room for improvement, 39–42
   using competency models to build questions, 59–62
Level 4
   analyzing and presenting data, 86–8
   asking the right questions, 81–6
   business metrics, 75–6
   calculating effect size, 92
   calculating leadership effect size, 97–9
   calculating the effect, 89
   defining "effected" population, 92
   defining productivity, 75–7
   designing, 78
   effect size, 88–93
   gathering data, 80–1
   highlighting impact of training when applied, 93–4
   how to collect, analyze, and report data, 73–5
   identifying "effect," 78–80
   leadership training and, 96–7
   overview, 12–13
   participants' impact, 76–7
   productivity differences, 87
   qualitative success stories, 99–100
   ramping up for Level 5, 93
   ROI, 94–5
   shifting accountability for success, 95–6
Level 5
   calculating benefit, 104–8
   calculating costs, 108–11
   calculating ROI for leadership training, 113–15
   direct benefits, 104–5
   how to collect, analyze, and report data, 103–4
   implementation cost, 108
   indirect benefits, 105–7
   invitation cost, 108–11
   overview, 13–15
   plugging into ROI equation, 111–13
   ROI formula, 104, 112
Level 6
   action and, 121–2
   analyzing and reporting results, 137–41
   benefits, 121–3
   creating transfer climate assessment, 123–37
   example of use, 144–6
   finishing bridge, 143–4
   future and, 121

Level 6—*Continued*
  how to collect, analyze, and report data, 117–21
  increase in ROI and, 123
  overview, 15–16, 117–21
  power of climate, 146–9
  scaling and scoring climate assessment, 134–7
  summing up, 141–3
  variability of results and, 122–3
  see also Transfer Climate Assessment

metrics
  behavior and, 7, 12
  defining, 49, 75–6, 169
  improving, 12–13, 47, 73, 81–3, 86, 96, 103, 114, 177
  Level 3 and, 12, 58, 60, 62, 169
  Level 4 and, 12–13, 39, 47, 73–7, 81–3, 93–4, 168–9
  Level 5 and, 14, 104–6, 125, 128–30
  observing, 50
  overstating, 91
  participants' impact on, 76–7
  quantitative, 99
  ROI and, 14, 180, 183, 188
  success and, 8

networking, 20

observable behaviors, training and, 50–1
one-on-one meetings, 54, 64, 68, 71, 124–5, 134, 139–40, 142, 144, 146–7, 159, 181, 195
organizational factors, 118–19
overall improvement, 67

people factors, 118–19
performance appraisals, 62, 126, 145, 147
performance metrics, 14, 76, 81–2, 96
Phillips, Jack, 10, 168
pillars, building, 8–10
post-test approach
  biggest takeaway, 31–2
  importance to role, 30–1
  intent to apply new knowledge, 31
  new knowledge gained from training, 29–30
  overview, 28–9

post-training evaluation
  Levels 1 and 2, 153
  Levels 3–6, 154–7
pre-test approach, 27–30, 41–3, 45–6
productivity
  defining, 75–7
  differences in, 87
  gains in, 97–101
  see also return on investment (ROI)
psychometrics, 88, 90

qualitative
  Level 1, 23–4
  Level 2, 11, 31–3, 35
  Level 3, 62, 67–72, 173
  Level 4, 99–100
quantitative
  Level 1, 20, 23–4, 171
  Level 2, 11, 32–3, 171
  Level 3, 12, 62–7, 69, 173, 175
  Level 4, 86, 99
  Level 6, 153

reaction and satisfaction, 10–11
  see also Level 1
recognition, 62, 68, 71, 100, 124–6, 128, 132, 139, 144, 146, 159, 175, 181, 195
  see also rewards
response distribution, 20, 22, 32, 64–5, 173
results, training and, 49–50
return on investment (ROI)
  benefit and, 108
  calculation of, 13, 108, 113–15
  defining business case and, 49–51
  environment and, 119
  formula, 104
  Level 2 and, 30
  Level 3 and, 12
  Level 4 and, 94–6
  Level 5 and, 13–15, 93, 103–4
  Level 6 and, 15, 121, 123–4
  metrics and, 14, 180, 183, 188
  plugging into ROI equation, 111–13
  pre-post design and, 45
  training and, 10, 77, 95, 111–15, 129
  see also Level 5
reviewing training content, 55, 60, 62

reviews
    of employees, 62, 105
    of survey results, 134
    of training, 21
rewards
    climate assessment and, 119, 124–6, 139, 141
    competency models and, 62
    expectation of, 144–5, 159, 182, 193
    improvements and, 132, 142, 175, 181, 183
    as "make or break" climate factor, 139
    as organizational factor, 119, 132
    see also recognition

safety nets, 94
sample size, 68, 85, 174, 177, 186
satisfaction
    customers and, 13, 75, 93, 100–1, 103, 106–8
    training participants and, 3–4, 10–11, 17, 25, 33, 35, 168, 170, 187
success stories, 62, 69–70, 94, 99–100, 134, 173
survey questions, scaling, 21–3

Target Impact Plan (TIP), 146–8
testimonials, 6, 31

time
    analysis and, 29
    collecting data and, 13
    measuring value of, 1, 11, 40, 108
    ROI and, 108–10
Transfer Climate Assessment
    applying training behaviors, 130–1
    commitment to organization, 133
    compensation and, 132
    creating, 123–4
    encouragement of peer groups, 128
    example document, 135–6
    factors for, 124
    linkage between training and metrics, 129–30
    one-on-one meetings to discuss training, 125
    opportunity to apply training, 129
    recognition and rewards, 125–6
    relevance of training, 131–2
    scaling and scoring, 134–7
    support and endorsement for training, 126–7
    supporting employee development, 130
    trying out behaviors without fear of consequences, 127–8
T-test, 88

variables, 46, 79–80, 88, 90, 138, 179